Women, Faith, and Work

Women, Faith, and Work

How Ten Successful Professionals Blend Belief and Business

Lois Flowers

Foreword by Thomas G. Addington and Stephen R. Graves

WORD PUBLISHING

NASHVILLE

A Thomas Nelson Company

Published by Word Publishing, a Thomas Nelson, Inc., company, P.O. Box 141000, Nashville, Tennessee 37214, in association with the literary agency of Alive Communications, Inc., 7680 Goddard Street, Suite 200, Colorado Springs, Colorado 80920.

Unless otherwise indicated, Scripture quotations are from the Holy Bible: New International Version®. Copyright © 1973, 1978, 1984 by International Bible Society. Used by permission of Zondervan Publishing House. All rights reserved.

Verses marked KJV are from the King James Version of the Bible.

ISBN 08499-4286-1

Printed in the United States of America
1 2 3 4 5 6 7 8 9 PHX 06 05 04 03 02 01

Contents

To Randy—my best friend and my biggest fan

Acknowledgments

FIRST AND FOREMOST, MANY, MANY, MANY THANKS to all the amazing women who are featured in this book: Susie Case, Pin Pin Chau, Karen Covell, Joyce Godwin, Allyson Hodgins, Carmen Jones, Dr. Sally Knox, Goldie Rotenberg, Jeanette Towne, and Bonnie Wurzbacher. You blessed me far more than I can ever express. Thank you for your transparency, your wonderful insights, your encouragement, and your prayers. I count it an honor to know each of you.

Thanks to Stephen Graves, Thomas Addington, and Sean Womack, cofounders of the Life@Work Co., for believing I could do this project before I ever thought it myself, for guiding me through the process, and for giving me the opportunity to be a part of your company.

Thanks to Stephen Caldwell, former executive editor at Life@Work, for all of your editorial advice and encouragement.

Thanks to Rosemary Walch for taking care of a million little details so I didn't have to worry about them, but most of all, for being such a wonderful source of support.

Thanks to Tonya Schein for coordinating all of my travel arrangements, handling part of the transcription work, and lining up our outside editorial committee.

Thanks to the rest of the Life@Work team, past and present, for your interest, support, and prayers.

Thanks to all the women who graciously reviewed parts of the book as it was being written: Sue Addington, Ann Arkins, Kathy Blank, Nandra Campbell, Nancy Caver, Karen Graves, Lynne Kenworthy, Sue Kyser, Beth Rogers, Andrea Scoggins, Sandie Sparks, and Kelly Sutterfield.

Thanks to Elizabeth Carlson, Rod Howard, Catherine Robertson, Dave Robinson, and Dr. Jean Wright for introducing Life@Work to some of the women in this book.

Thanks to the folks at Word Publishing, especially Mark Sweeney and Ami McConnell, for believing in this project and for guiding it to completion. Thanks to Holly Halverson for your expert touch at editing the manuscript.

Thanks to my parents, Robert and Angela Reimers, for encouraging me to develop my abilities and for giving me the solid spiritual heritage that helps me live out my own faith at work.

And thanks to my husband, Randy, for your unwavering support, confidence, and love.

Foreword

WOMEN HAVE LONG PLAYED IMPORTANT ROLES in business, but until the last sixty or so years, those roles were limited. Two things happened that changed all of that.

First, the Japanese attacked Pearl Harbor, and the United States, with its history for championing individual freedoms, joined the fray of World War II. Hundreds of thousands of women joined the work force as replacement workers for the men who had joined the military. Second, the microchip was invented, and the world began to shift to an information- and knowledge-based economy.

The way women viewed work and the way the culture viewed women as workers began to shift. Some women felt they had no option but to work. Cultural shifts such as the breakdown of the traditional family (which resulted in more single mothers raising children) and pressure toward two-income families (which resulted, in part, from increased taxation) brought scores of these women into the workplace. Others worked because they felt a societal obligation to do so, or because they felt called to contribute their unique gifts and skills. So fueled by new opportunities, an increasingly level playing field, and new cultural standards, the gender dynamics of the market-place changed forever.

It's a cultural shift that has challenged followers of Jesus in many ways and will continue to present challenges in the future. That's why we intentionally included women in our target audience when we launched *The Life@Work Journal* in 1998. Until then, the few publications that touched on faith and work were targeted almost exclusively to businessmen.

We founded the Life@Work Co. to help followers of Christ around the world integrate their faith and their work. This need for integration follows a general cultural trend toward a more holistic approach to life, which includes determining how work fits with family, church, community, and everything else.

As we began putting together the first issue of *The Life@Work Journal*, we operated under the presupposition that the experts at integrating faith and work are the practitioners in the marketplace—the people who spend their days in the professional trenches, rubbing shoulders with coworkers, employees, clients, vendors, customers, and patients.

As we began scouring corporate offices, hospitals, universities, office buildings, manufacturing plants, and sports complexes across the country for stories about men and women who were living out their faith at work, we found many high-profile men who fit the bill. But locating women with similar qualifications, we quickly discovered, was a bit more difficult.

In an increasing effort to identify women who are both leaders in the marketplace and committed followers of Christ, we asked our readers for recommendations. In the process, we learned about some incredible women whose stories we felt obligated to share with a wider audience.

That's the purpose of this book. It is *not* a book about women's issues or women's roles in today's culture, evangelical or otherwise. It *is* a book about what it looks like to be a woman and a follower of Christ in the twenty-first-century marketplace.

It is our hope that reading this book gives you an opportunity to view your work situation, decisions, attitudes, and actions through a different lens. You may not agree with everything you read; in fact, some of the opinions expressed by the ten women featured may even disturb you. But we strongly believe that a book like this has value because it raises possibilities and introduces perspectives that otherwise might be ignored. In addition to your being inspired by the women's stories, we trust their insights and experiences will help you forge your own faith-at-work philosophy and strategy.

When we developed the idea for this book with Word Publishing, we knew we needed to find a writer with some very specific qualifications. The writer had to be a woman. She had to be a thinker. She had to be a competent interviewer and journalist. She had to be someone with a good understanding of the Life@Work mission and values. And she needed to be an authentic follower of Jesus.

We looked all across the nation, but we kept coming back to someone close to home.

One of the most delightful and productive relationships we've developed in our Life@Work tenure has been with Lois Flowers, a former editor with *The Life@Work Journal*. She's not just a good writer; she's also the kind of fresh thinker who adds value to any topic that she covers. Lois weaves the anecdotes and insights of the women she interviewed for this book into simple-yet-comprehensive profiles that bring to life their struggles and successes and leave you feeling as if you've made ten new friends.

God calls all of us, men and women alike, to use our gifts and talents for him wherever we are. That's exactly what the women in this book are doing, and it is our prayer that their stories will encourage and motivate you in your quest to incorporate your faith into your work—whatever that work may be.

Thomas G. Addington and Stephen R. Graves
Cofounders, The Life@Work Co.

Introduction

AFTER A FEW MONTHS OF MEETINGS TO DETERMINE how The Life@Work Co. should approach a book for women on the integration of faith and work, my journey to complete this project began—physically and metaphorically—in Irvine, California.

It was late September 2000, and I had been invited to attend the inaugural meeting of Marketplace Women of Orange County, a group of women who had come together to encourage each other in their quest to integrate their personal, professional, and spiritual lives.

My role at the luncheon was minor; I was there simply to say a few words about *The Life@Work Journal* and to give the women a short overview of the book I was about to begin writing. Looking back, I cannot remember anything I said during my brief moments at the pódium. But I do recall—vividly, in fact—the words of the keynote speaker who followed me.

Judy Sweeney is a forty-four-year-old former management consultant who spent several years as president of the Orange County Edition of the *Los Angeles Times* before retiring to raise her two young children full-time. As she shared her life experiences pertaining to faith at work, she challenged the women in the audience to ask themselves two questions at the close of every day:

1. Whom did I work for today—God or someone else?
2. How did I respond to the situations I faced today?

With those convicting questions ringing in my ears, I set out to interview the women you're about to meet. How would they respond to such questions? I wondered. Would their daily answers reveal that their personal relationship with Jesus Christ was real, and that they were earnestly seeking to incorporate their life with Christ into their life at work? I suspected so, but I couldn't be sure until I actually talked with each of them.

They didn't disappoint me.

While several of the women grew up in church-going families, most of them did not come to understand what it truly means to be a follower of Jesus until they reached adulthood. But it didn't matter whether they came to that understanding in elementary school, in college, or several years into their career; each and every woman I interviewed has learned to look at her work through the lens of her faith in Christ. For some, the picture came into focus very early in life, while others needed the patient guidance of a trusted mentor or friend to fully realize their roles as believers at work.

Although this is not a book about the differences between men and women, one significant difference stood out as I traveled from city to city, interviewing the various women. Had I been interviewing men about faith at work, I'm guessing I would have met them at their offices and spent a few hours asking the many questions on my list. There would have been some personal interaction, but most of it would have been strictly business.

My experience with these women was very different. Keep in mind that none of them had met me in person before I showed up at their houses or offices (or, in a few cases, at the airport where they so graciously picked me up). I had interviewed one of them for a magazine article, so I was at least a bit familiar with her personality, but even she knew very little about me.

They weren't total strangers, of course. Most came highly recommended by friends of The Life@Work Co., and some had close ties to other members of the Life@Work staff. But with me, they were into unfamiliar territory.

But that didn't keep them from inviting me into their kitchens, dining rooms, or offices for an afternoon of intense, often extremely personal, conversation. Over cups of tea and glasses of sparkling water, these women shared their stories with me—stories marked by everything from amazing professional success and accomplishment to excruciating personal tragedy and sadness.

What do the personal stories have to do with how they live out their faith at work, you might ask? In some cases, not a thing. But in other cases, the difficult things these women (and, in some instances, their husbands) have faced in their personal lives have made such an indelible mark on who they are that it's impossible to ignore them. We are, after all, talking about integration here. Our professional lives are not separate from our personal lives. When a senior executive at a large corporation gives birth to premature identical twins who die a few hours later, that experience reaches the very core of who she is. At that point, she has two choices: she can either stuff all her emotions in a box and try to hide the whole experience from her colleagues (she didn't get to where she is by being a big softy, after all), or she can work through her grief and, after time, talk about her experience with others, knowing that by being vulnerable, she might be able to share her faith or encourage someone else who is going through a difficult time.

Interviewing ten women using basically the same list of questions can be a scary proposition for a writer. *What if all their answers start sounding alike?* I asked myself. *What if I get bored with the questions—and the women—before I'm finished? What if they all cite the same Scriptures, address the same struggles, and offer the same advice?*

I needn't have worried.

As I listened to them talk, I was struck by their heartfelt honesty. Not every woman would be willing to disclose her failures and weaknesses so candidly—at least not for publication—and most would never dream of openly discussing hard questions about their faith (although most of us would have to admit that we've asked the same questions privately). But these ten did both of those things. And that not only made their stories easier to write, it also gave me a more complete picture of who they really are.

We chose the women for this book carefully. We literally filled in a grid to ensure that we were including a cross section of ages, professions, ethnic backgrounds, current geographic locations, and family statuses. It's safe to say the women in this book are about as different from each other as any ten women could be. One spent her early years in a Jewish "ghetto" in the South Bronx, another on the prairies of Western Canada, yet another in Hong Kong, and still another in Bartlesville, Oklahoma. Some are married; some are single. Some have children; some do not. Some have pets (in my travels I had the pleasure of interacting with a very loving, very large "goldador"— half golden retriever, half yellow Lab—named Mason and a marmalade housecat named Undercat); some do not. Some live in opulent surroundings; others prefer a simpler environment. They represent an amazing mixture of talents and interests. One is a skilled artist who, rather than taking photographs, draws the scenery when she goes on vacations. Another is an avid golfer. And still another has been to—count them—eighty-three foreign countries.

But for all their differences, the women in this book have at least three very important things in common. They share a deep, abiding faith in Jesus Christ. They all are acutely aware that God has had his hand on their careers, from the time they accepted their first jobs as adults to the roles in which they find themselves now. And they all believe they have been called to their work, whether they spend their days operating on breast-cancer patients or leading the boards of internationally known nonprofit organizations.

You may not find yourself in the exact same position as any of the ten women in the book. But their stories still will affect your life profoundly.

Laugh with them. Cry with them. Be encouraged by them. Learn from them.

And keep Judy Sweeney's two questions—"Whom did I work for today — God or someone else?" and "How did I respond to the situations I faced today?"—in mind as you read. Chances are, you'll be able to apply several things from each chapter to your own life at work. But if you take only one thing away from reading this book, and that one thing helps you answer Judy's questions in a more Christ-honoring way, it will be worth every page.

Lois Flowers

1

Karen Covell
HOLLYWOOD PRODUCER

KAREN COVELL WAS THRILLED.

An independent producer in Hollywood, she had just been hired to work on MSNBC's one-hour celebrity profile show, *Headliners and Legends with Matt Lauer*. She had been involved with a variety of television and film projects throughout her twenty-year career in the entertainment business, but this was among the most visible. On top of that, it came along when she and her composer-husband were particularly thankful for the work.

But Karen's excitement quickly subsided when she received her first assignment. Instead of Billy Graham, whom she had placed at the top of her wish list of profile candidates, the show's executives chose Hugh Hefner, the founder and CEO of the Playboy empire.

Karen was extremely disappointed. A committed follower of Christ for more than two decades, she was appalled at the idea of highlighting the life and work of a person whose values were so diametrically opposed to her own. At the same time, she and her husband had spent many years encouraging other believers in the entertainment industry to be more bold about sharing their faith, and she simply couldn't ignore the fact that participating in this project might give her an opportunity to have a spiritual impact on Hefner. "I didn't want to be a part of it, but I had to be reminded that this was exactly why I have chosen to work in Hollywood and specifically what I had been praying for," she says.

As the associate producer, Karen didn't have much control over the content of the show; she was responsible for the technical aspects of hiring crews, lining up interviews, handling the budgets, and so on. But rather than keeping quiet, Karen decided to talk to the show's producer.

She knew that Hugh Hefner had been the subject of many profiles, most of which devoted a lot of airtime to such things as the seductive Playboy Mansion and the famous Playboy Bunnies. So she proposed an alternative. "This is your show, but I just had a thought," she told the producer. "Instead of exploiting a man who's been exploited so often, how about taking a different approach and focusing on why he became who he is? Let's look at his background—there has to be a reason why a man is driven to make the choices he's made."

As it turned out, Rick, the producer, also was a believer. When he received the assignment, he was just as horrified as Karen. So he went to his pastor for advice. "If you turn down the job," his pastor said, "*somebody* is going to do it. Would you rather do it and try to make a difference by what you *don't* include and by approaching it from your world-view, or would you rather let someone else produce a profile that features the same old exploitation story?"

Given that choice, the producer decided to take his pastor's challenge. He and Karen began working together, praying continually for the project and for Hefner. But when it came time to talk to Hefner in person, Karen balked. Going to the Playboy Mansion for the interview was the last thing she wanted to do.

Her husband, Jim, set her straight. "If you're praying for this man, and if you're wanting to have an impact on him, you go," he insisted. "You meet him, and you shake hands with him. And you pray for Rick the entire time he's doing the interview."

So she went.

Karen had done her homework, and she knew that when it came to theology, Hefner reportedly had worked out his own belief system to fit his lifestyle. But in keeping with her desire to touch him with the gospel somehow, she brought along a book—*Can Man Live without God?* by Ravi Zacharias (Word Books, 1996)—that she hoped to give to him while she was at the mansion.

She didn't get a chance to give Hefner the book while she was there. After the profile aired, however, she mailed it to him, along with a letter. She explained that she had been the associate producer of the show and that throughout the process of doing the program, she had been amazed at all of his accomplishments. In fact, Karen said, it seemed that the only thing Hefner hadn't yet done in his life was to embrace a personal God. "I know you *know* God," she wrote. "I know you know he's a *living* God, but I don't think you believe he's a *loving* God." After mentioning a bit of what she had learned about him, she then added, "My prayer for you is that you will be challenged and inspired to embrace the loving God. That, I believe, would be your last and greatest accomplishment."

A short time later, Karen received a personal note from Hefner. He thanked her for the book and for her kind words. He said he enjoyed his profile very much, and then he responded to her comments about God by saying that he had his own unique-yet-specific religious beliefs with which other people would not agree.

Karen was surprised that he answered her letter so quickly, but she wasn't disappointed by his reaction. "I thought, *That's quite fine*," she says. "I challenged him; I gave him the book; I laid out the whole understanding of who Jesus is in the letter. I thank the Lord for that opportunity, and now I continue to pray for him."

Missionary to the Entertainment Industry

To hear Karen tell this story, one might think she was born passing out gospel tracts. But that is far from the case. In fact, when she accepted Christ as a freshman theater-producing major at the University of Southern California, she did so on one condition: she would commit her life to Jesus only if she didn't have to tell anyone about him. Her reluctance was understandable. She had grown up in a family where the prevailing opinion was that religion and politics were two topics that you simply didn't discuss with other people.

So much for making deals with God.

As Karen grew in her faith and began her career, she became increasingly convinced that God *had* called her to be a missionary. But she wasn't called to the jungles of Africa. She was called to work in another mission field—the entertainment industry.

Eighteen years ago, she and her husband helped found a prayer group whose members meet once a month to pray for the industry, their work, and their colleagues. Now called PREMISE, this group's meetings attract seventy to eighty people. And for the last decade, the couple has been teaching a lifestyle evangelism class in their home that is geared specifically to entertainment industry professionals. Called "How to Talk about Jesus without Freaking Out," this class recently led to a book by the same title (Multnomah Publishers, 2000) that Karen and Jim coauthored with Victorya Michaels Rogers.

The Covells also speak frequently to college audiences, churches, and professional groups around the country, encouraging people of faith to view the entertainment business as a mission field. They're passionately proclaiming the late Bob Briner's message in his best-selling *Roaring Lambs* (Zondervan Publishing House, 1993) that believers shouldn't shy away from careers in the arts because it's a crucial place to be an influence for Christ.

Karen is fully aware that many people of faith would not feel comfortable working in the entertainment industry, but it was always a natural fit for her. Her father was a business owner by profession but an entertainer for fun, and her mother was an actress in her youth. So, growing up in a northern suburb of Chicago, Karen was immersed in a plethora of theatrical and musical experiences, from concerts and plays to ballets and operas. It's easy to see why this five-foot, two-inch, blond forty-two-year-old once wanted to be an actress herself. She's warm and bubbly. She's dramatic. She's animated. And she's a bundle of energy. "Jim says I always want to find all the Easter eggs—I don't want to miss anything in life," she says with a smile.

Although Karen seems ideally suited for the career she chose, she still occasionally is criticized for the work she does. When asked about her secret for handling her detractors, her answer is simple: "I don't think it's a secret; it's a calling. I *have* to be here. And I have to encourage others who I think have a strong faith to do the same thing."

Take, for example, a good friend who is a writer on a soap opera. "She has people flat-out tell her that is the wrong place to be: 'How can you dare to be a Christian and work in soap operas?' I keep e-mailing her and telling her, 'You're doing right; keep it up; this is great,'" Karen says. Why is she so adamant? It's like another producer friend once told her: his greatest ministry is in what he keeps *out* of his shows, versus the few things he gets to put in. "That's how I felt about the Hugh Hefner experience," she says.

Not everyone saw it that way, of course. When Karen was lining up crews for the Hefner interview, she wanted to bring as many believers to the mansion with her as possible. So she tried to recruit a cameraman whom she knew to be a follower of Christ. "He told me that he didn't believe this was the right thing for him to do," she says. "That confirmed to me what I believe—that our faith has to come out in a different way for each of us. He needed to stay away, and I needed to go in."

Chicken-Potpie Theology

When Karen was younger, she tried hard to integrate her faith into her work. Now, thanks to a powerful analogy she heard in a class, she looks at her life a bit differently. According to the teacher, many people of faith live their lives as if they were TV dinners, with separate compartments for church, friends, work, their children, their neighborhood, and so on. Each area of life is segmented, and they act differently in each one. But, he said, a believer's life should be like a chicken potpie, where everything is thrown into one bowl, mixed together, and covered with a crust. You can't separate the vegetables from the meat because the gravy holds them all together. "I thought, *That's it!*" Karen says. "I don't want to think about integrating my faith. I want it to be so much a part of me that I can't help it."

That's not to say Karen doesn't continually evaluate individual decisions and actions through the lens of her faith. One of the most significant ways in which her relationship with Christ impacts her work is through the projects that she and her husband (the two are partners in an independent television and music production company) turn down. "We have chosen to work in places that a lot of Christians would feel uncomfortable in," she admits, "and the line we draw might be different from that of some people. As we honor and respect other Christians' choices, we have our point where we draw our line too. There are projects that both Jim and I have been offered to work on that we just can't do."

Many years ago, for example, the Covells read in a trade newspaper about one of the youngest husband/wife directing-and-producing teams that had ever worked in Hollywood. Since Jim and Karen also work together, they decided to track down this couple and find out what kind of work they were doing, with the hopes that the four could collaborate in the future. Quite quickly, however, the Covells realized that the other couple primarily made R-rated films that went straight to video. At that point, Jim and Karen knew they couldn't work together. But they did want to maintain their burgeoning friendship because they really liked the couple, and they recognized that they might be able to have a spiritual impact on them.

When it came time for the young couple's next film, they naturally assumed that the Covells had pursued the friendship solely for work purposes because that was the only kind of relationship they'd ever had. "In a lot of businesses like ours, where it's so intense and where 'who you know' is so important, your friends are your work and your work is your friends," Karen says. "You really don't develop a friendship just for friendship's sake. It's all tied together with your career."

It would have been easier just to say that they were too busy, but when the Covells turn down work, they are committed to explaining, in a kind way, exactly why they can't do it. The couple wanted Karen to help produce their movie and they wanted Jim to write the music. But they asked Jim first, so he got the job of telling them no. He explained that he and Karen had no intention of insulting them or judging their project in any way, but that their faith and values simply prevented them from being able to work on it. "She immediately burst into tears, and he got defensive," Karen says. "And Jim thought, *There goes the friendship.*"

That was on a Friday. On Monday, the wife called Karen.

"How *are* you?" Karen asked, thinking, *She called me at least—that's a good sign.*

"I've had the worst weekend of my life," the woman replied. "I have spent all weekend walking around the house thinking, *Do I have any morals? Am I a moral person?*"

It turns out that the couple's conversation with Jim had triggered the woman to seriously question what she was doing. "It was incredible," Karen marvels, adding that the situation opened the door for Jim and Karen to really start talking to this couple about who they were and what they believed. "Now we even pray together," she says.

Total Dependence on God

Turning down work never is easy, especially for an independent producer like Karen. "When one job is over, I immediately start looking for the next one," she says. "It's the same with Jim. We don't have any financial security that way and it's very rough. That's where my faith is tested."

Sometimes, the testing can be difficult indeed. A couple of years ago, Karen and Jim both went through forty-day fasts. They experienced God's presence as never before, and they were both on "an absolute spiritual high." Then, literally within a week after Karen's fast ended, everything crashed around them: "The work just stopped. It was as if we turned the faucet off. There was no reason."

All the people they had worked for in the past had good reasons why they didn't need them anymore. Someone who had used Jim for years was now employed by another company that had a composer on staff. The company Karen had been working with had gone to more direct-marketing projects and wasn't doing television work anymore. Karen had a partner with whom she created movies for television, but that partnership ended because the woman got divorced and moved out of the country.

"My father was so concerned about us that he actually told me that maybe Jim and I needed to think about other careers," Karen says. "That was so hard. Dad said, 'It's not your fault; we know you have talent. But you've got a family; you've got to earn money.' And I said, 'Dad, this is my calling. I've got to believe that God is going to get us through this.'"

This dark, oppressive time dragged on for more than two years. But Karen can pinpoint the exact moment when she discovered at least one reason why God had allowed her to go through it. It was in August 1998, when the situation was at a particularly intense and awful stage. "I was on my knees and I said, 'Lord, I'm not going to pray anymore for circumstances to change,'" Karen says. "It suddenly became clear to me that I wanted everything around me to get better, but I didn't think about wanting *me* to get better. I then prayed, 'You don't have to change any circumstances—you just have to change me. And I have to be content regardless of what I'm going through. I have to find my joy in you in the darkest valleys. I can't be afraid; I can't be discouraged; I can't be frustrated. I have to find peace in you and not in my earthly circumstances.'

"That was a huge revelation," Karen continues. "At that point, I didn't expect anything we were going through to change—and it didn't. In fact, in some ways it became worse. But my response to it changed completely. I wasn't worried, but peaceful. I was trusting God that 'this too shall pass.' I actually had hope."

It was hope in the midst of despair. And the despair was about to deepen.

The following January, doctors discovered that the Covells' older son, Christopher, then eight, had a brain tumor the size of an orange growing in his cerebellum. Their concern was focused on Christopher, but their financial problems were magnified because they had no money to pay the deductible for the major surgery that their son required.

There was an answer, but it was a difficult pill to swallow. "First, our dear friends just poured money upon us. It was unbelievable what they did," Karen relates. "Second, the hospital came to me and said, 'We've seen your tax forms, and you can apply for California's state Medi-Cal to handle your deductible.' It was humbling, but because we hadn't worked for more than a year before that, we had no income on our tax forms."

Between the state assistance with medical bills and generous help from friends, the Covells made it through the crisis. "The Lord turned all of that around into such good and brought a community of believers around us that was so incredible. I get choked up thinking about it," Karen says. "He miraculously healed my son, and after we got through that wild month, boom! Work started."

The experience changed Karen's life. "It taught me total dependence on the Lord," she says. "I was told growing up that I could do anything if I just put my mind to it. I completely disagree with that now. I believe I can do anything that God wants me to do if I put my faith in him. And I can confidently face things that seem impossible because I now know the Lord will get me through them. I have an entirely new perspective. Every day—whether it is a good day or a bad day—I say, 'Lord, I have to depend on you. I can't do any of this without you. I can't fool myself and think because things are going well that I'm doing it—I can't.'

"Before the work stopped and Christopher became ill, I had been

absolutely believing the lie that I could make it through life successfully on my own," Karen continues. "I knew that the Lord was helping
me, and I believed that he was the one who ultimately got me through.
But I didn't really live it out that way because I was able to do things on
my own."

Relational Authenticity

Karen firmly believes that her work is a witness, that she has a
responsibility as a follower of Christ to do her best, no matter what the
job. But it is in the relational aspects of work that she really feels the pull
of her faith, from the way she interacts with people under her direction
to the way she relates to difficult coworkers.

She is a staunch advocate of servant-leadership, with Jesus as her primary model. "He served; he gave of himself; he put himself below others;
he didn't worry about the status of anyone," Karen said. Whether that
means consciously making sure she gets input from others before making decisions—and sincerely valuing their input—or cleaning the coffee
cups in the office kitchen even though she doesn't drink coffee, Karen is
willing to do it. "I want to go out of my way so that people see I care
about them as people and not just as someone I'm working with," she
says. "There's tremendous power in serving."

Women of faith in the marketplace walk a fine line between needing
to be tough and not wanting to act too masculine. It's sometimes difficult to take a stand without getting emotional, or to respond to problems
without getting hardened. "I like to be the servant, which is a much easier role for a woman to be in, but I also want to be taken seriously," Karen
says. "I can be the one who cleans the coffee cups because no one else
does it, but I also can be someone that my coworkers will listen to and
respect. It's an interesting dynamic."

With her slight build and effervescent personality, Karen knows
she doesn't really look or act the part of the typical aggressive businesswoman. But she's not afraid to put her feminine side to good use as she
deals with people at work, particularly men. She realizes, for example,
that many women are blessed with a keen sense of intuition, as well
as an ability to communicate in a gentle, nonthreatening manner. "I

understand the benefits that God has given women, and I take advantage of that," she says. "I think we have to be wise because we still aren't always as wanted or accepted in the workplace as men are. I'm not going to use the feminine traits the Lord gave me to flirt with some guy or to get personal attention, but I know I can say something in a way that's kind of cute and funny, yet gets my point across."

Once, the executive producer of the project she was working on was planning to do something that Karen knew wasn't good for the budget. She didn't think he wanted a woman telling him he was wrong, but she had to let him know the ramifications of his decision. So she went to see him.

"You know, here's a thought," she told him. "It might not work, but if we do it this other way, then we could save some money to go out and do something nice for the staff afterward."

By using a lighter touch to suggest an alternative, Karen achieved the result she needed. "When he came back to me, it became his idea, and that's okay," she says. "It doesn't have to be my idea, as long as the needed goal is accomplished. It's something that happens a lot with men, more so than with women: the ideas need to be theirs, the credit needs to be theirs, the sense of control needs to be theirs. And I've learned as a woman that I can be a lot more in control when I let them think they are. Some people think it's manipulative, but I believe God gave women that ability to get our ego out of the way so that we can get more done. That's the power of the woman in the workplace: if we don't worry about the credit or who's in charge, we get a lot more accomplished."

When it comes to dealing with difficult people, Karen tries to remember that everybody has a story. If someone is especially hard to deal with, there's always a reason for it. As she looks back over her career, she remembers one such case, especially because it's when she failed miserably only to have God step in and save the situation.

Several years ago, Karen was producing the Eighth Annual Women in Film Festival in Los Angeles, a large event that showcases the work of female filmmakers. One of the women she had hired to help with administrative work turned out to be a relentless problem. Betty (not her real name) was rebellious, stubborn, and sometimes downright nasty. As time went on, Karen grew more and more frustrated with her. "Betty wasn't doing her job; she was sarcastic and rude; she would slam doors; she had a horrible temper," Karen says. "I knew I had made a very unwise choice in hiring her."

The situation reached the boiling point late one evening. Karen had instructed Betty to make a delivery and then to report back to her. Karen, who was working with Jim in their home office that night, didn't hear from Betty, so she left a message for her. When Betty finally called back, Karen was on the phone with someone else so Jim ended up being the go-between.

The three-way conversation went something like this:

"Why didn't you call?"

"Oh, no one was there and I didn't even bother delivering it. I'll do it tomorrow."

"I told you this had to be there tonight. How could you not deliver it when that was your whole point in going?"

That was all Betty had to hear. She started yelling—at Jim since he was the one on the phone with her—about how she'd had enough of working for the film festival, that it was a rotten place to work, and so on.

Jim relayed the woman's responses to Karen. "You know what? You tell her if she's not happy here just not to come back," Karen shot back.

"Fine, I won't," Betty said before hanging up.

When Jim hung up his phone and Karen hung up from her other call, the realization of what they had just done hit them full force.

Karen tried to call Betty back, but she wouldn't answer the phone. The next day, she didn't come to work. Karen tried to reach her by phone again, but to no avail. In the meantime, she felt increasingly terrible about how she had handled the situation. "First of all, Jim never should have been a part of it," she admits today. "And second of all, I absolutely shouldn't have fired her like that. I should have had her come in and talk through the problems. I knew it, and it was awful."

Betty knew Karen was a believer, which made her feel even worse because she felt she had been a bad witness. "So I started to call her every few days just to say I cared about her, that I was very sorry, and that when she was ready to forgive me, I hoped she would," Karen says.

A few months later, just when Karen was about to give up "bugging" her, Betty finally called back. "Can we please have lunch?" Karen asked.

"Okay, I'm ready now," she replied.

That's when the rest of the story came out. Betty had grown up in a "religious" home where she was abused and sexually molested. Since then, she had become entrenched in the gay lifestyle. "She was wounded and hurt and angry at God and everyone else," Karen explains. "She said she had never had anyone care about her and be so persistent to keep calling like that, and she finally felt it was safe to open up to me."

That day at lunch, Karen watched God turn her failure into a miracle. "Here I was a few months later hearing Betty say, 'I want to get back to God; I need him; my life is a mess;'" Karen relates. "And I wanted to help because I had come to really love her."

The two began meeting to read the Bible, and Betty eventually recommitted her life to the Lord, went to seminary, and became a pastor. It was an amazing outcome, Karen realizes: "And it happened because I made such a horrible mistake on my own that I had to turn it over to God. He worked it out for good in a way that I never could have."

The Whole Truth

Karen is committed to living out biblical ethics in her daily work. But when it comes to taking a stand vocally, she faces an intriguing predicament. In her extremely competitive industry, it's common for people to rationalize unethical or immoral decisions based upon the fact that they need a paycheck. "They have separated it from even being a moral decision—it's a survival choice," Karen says. "Morality really does not even come into play with a lot of people. So when I look at a situation and deal with it as a moral issue, there are people in this industry who can't even relate to that."

For many years, Karen has been representing Jim in his music career. She makes calls for him when she learns about a movie that needs a composer, she negotiates deals, she handles the contracts, and so on. She has known one particular studio music supervisor for years, and although they have a good working relationship, he has yet to hire Jim for anything.

This has been very frustrating for Karen, but she got her chance to confront the music supervisor when Jim was up for a TV movie at the same studio. "It was the perfect time to call him because now I could say, 'Hey, look, a producer has approached Jim for a movie at your own studio, so you've got to hire him,'" Karen says.

Karen put in the call to the guy, all fired up and ready to state her case. But before he called her back, the producer of the TV movie called and said he had chosen someone else to do the music.

When the music supervisor finally called, Karen was still fired up. She told him that Jim was up for a TV movie at his studio so she thought it was about time he started hiring him. "Well, I knew at that moment that Jim hadn't gotten the job, but I didn't tell this guy," Karen confesses. "I wanted him to know that my composer was being pursued at his studio and darn it, he should be hiring him. We had always had this kind of repartee, but I was frustrated and I just wanted to lay it on him."

Finally, the music supervisor relented. "Okay, okay. Send me another CD of Jim's," he told her.

As soon as Karen got off the phone, conviction set in. "I thought, *I can't believe I just lied to him.*" The realization was too painful too ignore. "I decided that I had to call him back, tell him that I lied, and apologize."

So she did. When he answered, she said, "David, I lied to you."

"What are you talking about?"

"Well, I told you Jim was up for this movie and he was, but I knew he had lost it before you called back and I didn't tell you that."

"Oh, it doesn't matter; everybody does it."

As hard as Karen tried to convince him otherwise, the music supervisor would not acknowledge that she had misled him in any way. Karen knew the guy didn't tell the truth all the time himself, so he wasn't about to let her admit that she had lied. "He did not want this to become a moral conversation," she says today. "If I told him that I was wrong, then he would have had to acknowledge that he was wrong. So he wouldn't believe it—he was defending himself as he was defending me."

Karen never did convince the man that she was wrong, but that was okay. She let him know where she stood, and it was up to him to handle it. Because of situations like this, however, it's easy to see why she's sometimes careful about expressing her morality. "I will not compromise in it, but I might hesitate before bringing it up to make sure that I handle it wisely, especially in the face of opposition."

Redirected Ambition

When Karen was younger, her primary goal was to produce Broadway plays and Academy Award–winning feature films. Today, however, that intense desire is gone. "My career ambition has become less and less as I focus it for the Lord," she says. "I see my refocused priorities and goals as a miracle. I never would have believed that my career ambition would dissipate—it was absolutely my driving force. And it was working; I was really moving."

She does, however, still struggle with comparing herself to other people. "When I see other people who have really accomplished something, my first question is always, 'Okay, how old are they?'" she says. "If they're older than I am, I'm fine. If they're younger than I am, I want to know, 'Well, do they have a relative in the business or something?'"

Despite an occasional comparison crisis, Karen's primary ambition now is to please Jesus. "If the opportunity comes up to do something and it turns out great, I'll be absolutely thrilled, but it's not my desire now," she says. "I still want to use my gifts for the Lord, and I love working. But I was shocked at how having children changed me. My kids are my two feature films; they're my eternal projects.

"I want my children to follow the Lord—I don't want them to waver," she continues, referring to Christopher, now ten, and Cameron, six. "I don't want to force them into a relationship with Jesus, but to have it be so much a part of their hearts and souls that they never depart from him. And that takes a lot of time and commitment on all our parts."

Working independently, usually on short-term projects, has given Karen the flexibility she needs to fulfill her calling in the marketplace, and as a wife and mother. She works out of an office behind her modest home in Studio City, California, so that she is available to help her kids with their homework and accompany them on field trips.

But she feels pressure from some family and friends who think she should not work at all and others who think she should take long-term, full-time production work. She recently took a leave of absence from *Headliners and Legends with Matt Lauer* to finish a book of salvation stories called *The Day I Met God* (Multnomah Publishers, 2001). When she left the show, a few friends made it very clear to her that they thought she had done the right thing, while others were surprised she put such a great career opportunity on hold. She responded with the belief that every person—and every family situation—is different. "I think we have to do what's right for our own family," she says today. "Jim and I believe that God is the One who supplies the income for our family, not either one of us. So if the Lord gives me a job and doesn't give Jim one, he can spend time with the boys and I can work, and then we can go back and forth. We're very much a team in that way."

Karen's husband and boys also are her main measuring sticks for making sure her life is in balance. When she gets terribly busy, her husband and children are the easiest priorities to push aside—"because I know they love me, I know they will understand." At times like that, a comment such as "Mommy, are you going out *again*?" or "Can't you *ever* play handball with me?" is a sober reminder that she's out of whack. "I keep praying, 'Lord, keep me in balance. I'll think I've failed today because I haven't done every single thing on my list, but you just have me get done what you want, and I'll trust that that's all that I needed to do today.'"

Because of her commitment to her children, Karen has turned down jobs that could have been a big boost to her career. In late 1999, she declined an opportunity to produce a movie—her first feature film—because it required three months on location in Maine. "If my career ambition had still been my main priority, I would have taken it in an instant," she says. And instead of being an associate producer on *Headliners and Legends*, she could have been a producer, which meant that she would have been able to create and write the shows herself. "That work is incredibly time consuming," she explains. "I realized that if I did that, it would be all I could do. I couldn't be involved with my children or my husband or my ministry—all three of those would have had to go. And I wasn't willing to do that."

A Lesson in Contentment

Although Karen is confident that the family choices she has made in her career have been the right ones, she has at times struggled with contentment—particularly when it comes to the automobiles in her life. But as he so often does, God has used this seemingly insignificant struggle to teach her a valuable lesson about what's really important.

During the time when she and Jim didn't have any work, they got seriously behind financially. So they decided to turn in their leased Ford Explorer and buy a cheap, used car for cash. "If I was not a Christian, I don't think I would have done that," Karen admits. "I think I would have figured out a way, by hook or by crook, to keep that fun, impressive car."

After all, in the entertainment industry, image is everything. You have to look as if you're making money in order for someone to hire you because no one wants to hire a down-and-outer. "It's absolutely the world's way," Karen says. "But as Christians, we cannot work by the world's rules. It doesn't work for us."

The couple already had one old car, a little Toyota hatchback that Jim purchased used before they married in 1984. So while they were trying to figure out what kind of second car to buy, they got a call from Jim's father. It turned out that he had a friend who was trying to get rid of a car that his mother had owned. The car, a 1989 Buick, was in mint condition and had only thirty-five thousand miles on it. And the owner wanted a paltry forty-five hundred dollars for it.

When Karen was growing up, her father had traded in one of his cars for a new one every other year, so to her a new automobile was a sign of a successful family. On top of that, she was used to driving a trendy SUV. So the Buick, though cheap, wasn't a very attractive choice.

Practicality won out. Sight unseen, the Covells sent the money and went to get their "new" wheels. "The minute I saw this car, I burst into tears," Karen confesses. "I hated it. I said, 'No one under sixty-five drives this car! How can I bring this car home?'"

She did bring it home, and she did drive it. But for weeks, she was so embarrassed by the car that she tried to park it in an obscure place whenever she had an appointment so nobody would see her getting out of it.

Three years later, however, she still has the Buick (nicknamed "Hercules the Party Car" by her sons). And although she still jokes that she has yet to see another person under sixty-five driving a similar vehicle, she has no immediate plans to give it up. "It's been an incredible growing experience for me," she says. "The car hasn't stopped me from getting any jobs; it hasn't made anybody not like me. I am living by God's rules, we're catching up financially, and nothing horrible has happened."

Nothing horrible that God hasn't ultimately worked out for good, that is. Whether it be something as minor as a stodgy car or as major as a brain tumor, Karen clearly sees how she's grown and benefited from the challenges she has faced in her life. And if she can use those experiences to encourage others or to help them come to know Christ in a personal way, she's not about to keep them to herself.

"There is a purpose for hard times," she says. "I now have a better answer for nonbelievers when they ask, 'How can I believe in a God who lets bad things happen?' I can say with total commitment, 'He's got to let things happen because we don't turn to him otherwise. We sometimes think we don't need God if we're not in a place where the only way to look is up.'"

2

Dr. Sally Knox

BREAST SURGEON

WHEN SALLY KNOX DECIDED THAT SHE wanted to be a doctor when she grew up, it came as a complete surprise to everyone who knew her.

Although she was a good student who excelled at math and science, she just didn't seem to be the doctor type. She was shy. She didn't have good people skills. She was insecure. And she certainly didn't appear to have the stamina necessary to make it through medical school. So it was no wonder family and friends in her hometown of Bartlesville, Oklahoma, often reacted to her career choice by saying, "You, a doctor? I don't think so."

But Sally, who had accepted Christ at the tender age of nine, decided to ignore conventional wisdom—and her own personal doubts—because she truly believed that God was calling her into medicine. Even so, when she received her acceptance letter to medical school, she thought it was a mistake. She genuinely expected to get another letter a few days later stating that some embarrassing error had been made, that she had not been accepted after all.

That second letter never came. So, full of fear, Sally embarked on a journey through medical school at the University of Texas at Galveston.

Sally's fears were unfounded—she thoroughly enjoyed her studies. But when it came time to choose a residency program, many of the old misgivings resurfaced. She had loved her surgical rotations, and she couldn't ignore the nudging in her heart to go into that specialty. But she struggled with that option because of the self-sacrifice and long hours involved. The fact that she didn't fit the stereotype of a surgeon also gave her second thoughts. She simply didn't have the aggressive, hard-hitting, commando-type personality that many surgeons have; her compassionate nature seemed better suited for some other field. On top of that, she knew that surgical residencies were extremely strenuous, and she didn't think she had the physical strength to make it through five years of training followed by a lifetime of medical demands.

Once again, Sally wasn't alone in her doubts. Some of her medical school classmates were equally skeptical. "Surgery didn't seem very lady-like to them," she says today. "Nor did it seem compatible with raising a family, which was something I desired, or any semblance of a normal life."

But, as had become her custom, Sally decided to go with her heart. "I don't think God bangs us on the head and says, 'I want you to apply for a surgery residency.' It was just something that I felt I was supposed to be doing. I decided that I would apply and interview, and then see what happened. My plan was that I wouldn't get accepted, and then I would feel justified in pursuing something else."

Had her classmates been standing nearby when Sally opened her acceptance letter for the surgical residency, they would have seen her turn white as a sheet. A positive answer was not part of her plan. "Sheer terror gripped me," she confesses. "I had to think fast. What was I going to do? I couldn't come up with any solution other than to show up for the training."

Sally quickly discovered her knack for surgery. She had always enjoyed painting and playing the piano, and she was able to use those technical skills in the operating room. "There are a lot of tedious parts to surgery that fit me very well," she says. "I love to be meticulous, so for me it was similar to music or art. Performing surgical procedures is very much like sculpting or art."

As Sally neared the end of her surgical residency, her program director asked if she was interested in continuing her training for one more year to study breast oncology. As a general surgeon who also was a woman, Sally knew she would be seeing quite a few breast-cancer patients. On top of that, she'd already been in surgical training for five years—one more didn't seem like an unreasonable commitment. So she went to Dallas to study breast-cancer management and care. While there, she was recruited to devote her practice exclusively to breast surgery. "My mentors and the surgeons who were training me felt that there was a real need because the patients were looking for a woman surgeon," she explains.

That was fourteen years ago. Today, that shy, fearful medical student is one of the most respected breast surgeons in Dallas. Now forty-six, Sally is on the medical and teaching staffs at Baylor University Medical Center. She's an active member of the Christian Medical and Dental Associations, the American College of Surgeons, and other professional organizations. She's spoken at numerous meetings on breast carcinoma and other topics. And she has been actively involved in both medical and church-related mission projects to Russia and Eastern Europe.

Sally, who is single, still doesn't have that stereotypical surgeon's personality, but she is determined and tenacious when she is working to meet a goal that's important to her. Whether that involves looking for ways to provide medical care to women who can't afford it or performing surgery with excellence, she is constantly aware that her actions are a reflection of her Creator. And she is acutely cognizant of the fact that she is where she is, not because of her own strength, but because God has placed her there. "I would have never in my wildest imagination thought I would be doing what I'm doing now," she says. "I didn't believe in me as much as he did."

The Best and the Brightest

Over the years, Sally has made it a priority to equip herself to practice medicine as well as she possibly can because she believes God's people should be outstanding in their fields. There's biblical precedent for this: Joseph's, David's, and Daniel's contemporaries recognized these godly men as excelling in their work. Such skillful performance, she believes, must precede any verbal testimony of Christ's presence in her life: "We don't have a witness at all until we represent excellence in our work, attitudes, and behavior. I really believe that God will make us excellent or help us to achieve it as we look to him.

"To that end, my goal is to learn to be responsive to him," she explains. "When I considered Jesus feeding the five thousand, it occurred to me that if the lad with the fish and bread had brought twice as much—say four fish instead of two—it would have made little difference in the miracle that followed. Thousands were fed as those fish multiplied to meet the need. That says to my heart that it is not so much my abilities that make a difference in this world, but Jesus' abilities working through me. If I were twice as smart or gifted, it would not significantly impact what he can do through me. That is why the glory is his. He takes the little I bring to him and multiplies it to meet needs. That is the excellence that opens the door to ministry."

When patients who are followers of Jesus ask Sally for a referral to a Christian specialist, she encourages them to look instead for the best doctor for their needs. "When they're seeking out a physician, what they're wanting to purchase is medical care, so what they want is a recommendation for the best medicine there is," she said. "It's wonderful if that physician also happens to be a Christian because that will give the patient and physician a certain rapport to start with. But God is able to use physicians of every persuasion to touch his children. Patients can trust God to take them through whatever illness or medical situation they're facing. Physicians and other healthcare workers are simply some of his tools."

Sally isn't in a group with any other physicians, so she can promote her practice however she wants. But she has been very careful not to make her Christianity a gimmick. That requires sensitivity to the religious preferences of each individual patient. "Christ is reaching out to non-Christians through my hands and voice," she says. "The key to ministry is being alert and sensitive to patient needs and to show the highest respect regardless of differences of beliefs."

Biblical Business Handbook

Although Sally doesn't advertise that she's a follower of Christ, she is committed to operating her practice according to biblical principles. For instance, she believes that the Book of Proverbs is a treasure trove of guidance for people who want to do business God's way. Take Proverbs 22:1: "A good name is more desirable than great riches; to be esteemed is better than silver or gold."

How does that translate into practical terms? Simply stated, it means that people are more important than money and other things, Sally says. In her profession, for example, that might involve taking a minute to listen to an employee rather than rushing on to the next paying patient.

Although valuing people more than profits sounds like an easy concept to grasp, it actually is a lofty and deeply complex standard, Sally says. "Making a profit supersedes all other priorities in the secular mindset. One book I scanned recently about climbing the ladder in business took the first chapter to explain why one should always take the job that pays the most. This thinking becomes so ingrained that we don't even recognize it in our behavior and decisions."

As the owner of her own practice, Sally knows firsthand that making a profit is necessary in any business; without it a company will not succeed. But money is not the most important thing. "Matthew 6 tells us to seek first God's kingdom, and all these things will be ours as well," she says. "Those who feel that spiritual principles are not applicable to real-life business may argue that God doesn't pay the rent. I would say that God is the only One who has ever paid the rent. What we see as ours is actually his. And it is only with his guidance and help that any company has become profitable, regardless of whether the CEO acknowledges that or is aware of it."

The wisdom Sally has gleaned from Scripture impacts the way she relates to people who work in her office. "The way I treat them affects the way they treat the patients," she says. "If I'm disagreeable or hard to get along with, then they may pass that on to the patients. But most important is the fact that the people to whom I have to be a good witness—who know if I walk the walk and talk the talk—are the people I work with day in and day out. If they don't have a respect for my faith, then my faith is of no use."

Another biblical principle that Sally believes goes against conventional business thinking has to do with how a person gets to the top. Some schools of thought suggest that a person achieves success by stepping on others and looking out solely for his or her own interests. But Scripture teaches that God's way to the top is to first become a servant. So Sally looks for ways to serve others rather than promote herself. A few years ago, for example, she had an opportunity to advance into a particular position left vacant by another surgeon when he moved. The temptation would have been to climb the ladder herself, but Sally wanted another surgeon whom she felt was gifted and who greatly desired the responsibility to have a chance at it. So she stepped out of the way, he received the promotion, and he has excelled in the position.

By studying the Bible, Sally has become increasingly aware of the importance of training her mind and guarding her conversation at work. "If we're not aware of our talk, we migrate back to the easy things to gripe about, like the weather," she says. "Have you ever noticed that when you get on an elevator, it's expected that you have some sort of negative comment? 'I wish it wasn't raining.' 'Oh, it's too hot.' It's almost humorous! If you say, 'I'm having a great day' or 'I love the weather,' it may even feel awkward! People aren't expecting that and don't know quite how to respond."

As Sally thought about this, she was reminded of a verse from Psalms, which says, "O magnify the LORD with me, and let us exalt his name together" (Ps. 34:3, KJV). "As I pondered this, I realized that magnifying had to do with what my mind was thinking about over and over," she says. "If I magnify the Lord, my thoughts are on the wonderful things he has done. So I began to pay attention to what my mind was doing all day long. To my surprise, I found it rarely magnifying the Lord. Instead, it was preoccupied with an upcoming project, or a personnel problem, or a stack of charts that I needed to work through."

When Sally made this discovery, she decided to purposely and intentionally direct her mind to God's greatness several times a day. "It can be as little as remembering how he helped me find my keys yesterday and thanking him again, or as significant as remembering some of the awesome things he did in the Bible," she says. "This requires practice, just as practicing the piano or preparing for the Olympics does. But I have also begun to notice what wonderful fruit it produces in me: greater calm, more joy, better concentration. I have become much more aware of how much our daily environment beckons us to doubt and worry. We are literally bombarded with negative input all day long. But God offers an oasis of hope. Rarely do we fully appreciate how his principles work. But when we deliberately choose to practice them, fruit starts to appear that is often surprising."

The Power of Prayer

Through experience and her continued study of Scripture, Sally has a pretty good handle on what it means for her to incorporate her faith into her work. It hasn't always been that way, however. When she was in medical school, she was desperately trying to understand what it meant to be a follower of Christ who practiced medicine. For a few months she decided that she should pray with every patient. "It didn't matter if he or she was Hindu or what," she said. "This created a number of awkward situations, and I finally gave up on that, realizing that it wasn't working out too well. I laugh now, but I know I bounced all over the map trying to figure out what was expected of me as a Christian physician."

These days, Sally is much more sensitive to the spiritual openness of her patients. It's not too difficult to discern whether they might be receptive to prayer; the religious preference line on their new patient information sheet often is a good indication of their spiritual leanings. She might pray with one in ten patients, often those who are at a particularly traumatic stage of their diagnosis or treatment. Once, for example, a patient came to her office about two weeks after she was treated for breast cancer. Both she and her husband were at their wits' end—the patient hadn't been able to sleep for two weeks, and she was overcome with anxiety and stress. "I can't take another five minutes! Somebody's got to help me," she told Sally.

The patient had suffered similar problems in the past, but none of the medications she had taken before were yielding any relief this time. "Her husband was looking at me, almost wide-eyed, saying, 'Do *something* for her!'" Sally says. "I didn't know anything to do but pray. As a medical professional I didn't really have another pill. So I said, 'Let's just pray about this.' And I did."

The woman called Sally a few days later to tell her that the prayer had broken her fear and she was sleeping again—much to Sally's relief. "I thought, *Phew!* I could have referred her to a psychiatrist, and had it gone on for much longer, I would have done that. But I went with a gut feeling that this woman needed the peace that only Jesus can give. I was taking a risk there. I gave her what I felt she really needed, and God healed her anxiety, returning her to normal functioning. She became one of my most grateful patients, and the prayer meant far more to her than my surgical expertise."

Six months later, the patient and her husband stopped by to give Sally something they had written about how lifesaving that moment was for them. "That was a real blessing to me," she says. "It confirmed to me that taking the risk was worth it."

A few years ago, a reporter from *Good Housekeeping* interviewed Sally for a story on praying with patients. When the reporter asked if prayer works, Sally's answer was simple. "No," she told him, "it's not prayer that works, it's Jesus. It is an important distinction."

"There may be those who feel that the act of praying has some mystical effect that brings calm or a beneficial feeling to the person praying," she says. "Prayer is only the message. What matters is to whom that message is sent. For example, if I were an employee of a company, perhaps working in the mailroom, and I needed a new piece of equipment, there would be nothing particularly special about the piece of paper requesting the piece of equipment. What would make an enormous difference is the person to whom I sent the memo. If I sent it to a fellow mailroom worker, I would have little chance of getting the equipment. If, instead, I had access to the CEO and I sent the memo to him, I would have a much greater chance of receiving the equipment."

Meeting Needs

Sally is passionate about meeting the needs of her patients, whether they are spiritual needs that she can address with prayer or physical needs that require extensive surgery. And because she views her surgical skills as a gift from God, she believes she should use them to help all women who come to her, including those who are un- or underinsured. But this isn't as simple as it may sound. "I repeatedly encountered situations where women needed my medical services but couldn't access them because they also needed hospital care or expensive tests," Sally says. "Those things were beyond my purview to help. After encountering a thirty-year-old woman who was bright, productive, taking care of kids, and holding down an outside job—but uninsured when she developed breast cancer—I felt I had to at least try to make a difference."

This particular woman had been forced to ask friends, relatives, and whoever else she thought might be able to help for financial assistance to begin her treatments. "This, on top of the trauma of discovering breast cancer at such an early age," Sally says. "A cancer diagnosis generally means that purchasing health insurance is out of the question for several years. So she was stuck."

Shortly after hearing this woman's story, Sally began calling on former breast-cancer patients who she knew could identify with the pain and fear that this thirty-year-old patient faced. Together, they developed a nonprofit organization, the Bridge Breast Center, to help other women in similar situations. "I was touched by what I felt was the obvious hand of God on the project as professional women, such as an attorney, a journalist, an accountant, and many other gifted women, became involved," Sally says.

Sally's desire to see needs met also helps her maintain a Christ-centered view of her competition. Once, for example, she noticed that quite a few of the doctors who had been referring patients to her had begun to refer them to other physicians. This was an unsettling discovery and Sally's first inclination was to wonder, *Am I treating patients ineffectively?* Further research revealed that doctors were doing this for the simple reason that Sally's office was so busy that patients often had to wait six to eight weeks for an appointment. "I realized that quicker access to care was a good thing for patients, and that was what was important," she says. "It did prompt me to make some changes that helped the most urgent patients to get in quickly. But it also humbled me to see and accept my own limitations. I had to realize it wasn't about me. It's about getting the women taken care of."

Sally's attitude toward competition in general also is at wide variance with the norm. "Hospital systems are very competitive with one another, as are physicians and departments within medicine," she says. "But when I hear of other hospital systems improving their breast services, I consider that a good thing. That means that patients will get better or quicker care, and that is positive. The temptation is to feel threatened: *Perhaps the hospital across town will attract many of my patients and have a negative impact on my own practice.* Rather than take that viewpoint, I prefer to concentrate on doing the very best I can for my patients and c contributing to continuous improvement of services offered at my own institution. My reasoning is that you can't have too much of a good thing. If others are offering good things as well as myself, all the better for patients."

Many of Sally's associates consider this perspective naive, she admits: "They are waiting for me to catch up to understanding current business strategies. But I have my information from an excellent source. The Bible teaches me to put the needs of others first and to serve. If God is truly my source, and I am obeying his principles, then he will give me wise business strategies. Savvy planning and good strategy are important, but it's maintaining the right priorities that is the challenge. The right strategy can't be self-serving. It must put the needs of patients first."

A Woman in a Man's Field

When Sally was in medical school, only about 10 percent of the people in her class were women. Now, the male/female ratio of medical students is nearly equal, but it varies depending on the specialty. Women physicians often are attracted to such specialties as pediatrics, obstetrics and gynecology, and family practice. Although there are more female surgeons than ever before, surgery is still not heavily populated by women.

From medical school on, Sally always has made it a point not to compete with the men or try to be "one of the boys." "I truly feel that God called me to do what I do," she says. "He knew I wasn't a man, so he apparently intended for women to be involved in medicine. That understanding helped a great deal when I was in training. Early on the guys really tested me—they wanted to know if I could keep up and carry my load. After two or three months, that issue was settled. In fact, they actually became protective of me. I was amused by it because it told me that I could be a woman, I could be a physician, I could be good at what I was doing, and it didn't have to threaten the guys. They were happy to have me around."

Sally has watched many women try to gain acceptance in a man's world by doing all they could to be just like the men. But it's a lot more fun to do just the opposite, she says. "I enjoy fully embracing the differences and using them to my advantage in an uplifting and healthy way. For me, the surest way to gain respect is to give it to others. This won't work with every person. The attitudes of others may be entrenched or there may be other dynamics playing a part. But undermining others is never helpful, and I don't want another person's problem to become my own."

Some women physicians are resentful, Sally believes, because they think they have been excluded from certain professional opportunities simply because they are women. Unfortunately, that does happen, although it seems to be slowly changing for the better, Sally says. But exclusivity can go both ways. Several years ago, for example, a group of physicians proposed an all-women doctors group that would cater to the needs of women patients. Although this sounded like a good idea at first, to Sally it was more of the same behavior that the women objected to initially. "They were fighting an attitude they didn't like with the same attitude," she says. "The only way to fight gender bias is not to engage in it in any form."

This isn't always a popular approach. Sally recently had the opportunity to moderate and speak on a breast-cancer panel at a prestigious meeting. The other speakers she selected to be on the panel were excellent educators, articulate speakers, and knowledgeable physicians and researchers. But the fact that they also happened to be men drew criticism from other women surgeons. "Although I would gladly have included women on the panel, I would not select strictly based on gender," Sally says. "There are many gifted women who undoubtedly could have done as well, but I did not have their names at the time I chose the panel. I make it a habit to always keep an eye out for gifted women as well as men to whom I could possibly give a hand up some day."

Sally also goes against the grain among many women physicians when it comes to her pro-life stance. "In some women's professional organizations, they assume that if you're an intelligent woman with an education, and particularly if you're a physician, it goes without saying that you're pro-abortion. They don't even ask the question. They almost view you as an anomaly or suggest you're abandoning women if you are pro-life. That makes it tough. That means that many of the professional women's organizations have values 100 percent contrary to my values. Consequently, I'm not very welcome there. That is one reason the Christian Medical and Dental Associations have been such a blessing to me. They provide opportunities to meet and know professionals with whom I share common values."

Setting Limits

One of the most difficult challenges facing any physician, male or female, is finding ways to keep work from taking over his or her whole life. "In medicine there is always somebody who needs you right now, today," Sally says, "someone who just found a lump yesterday, or just got a needle biopsy back that showed cancer."

Sally typically does thirteen or fourteen surgeries during her two or three days in surgery each week, and she sees anywhere from ten to forty-five patients each of the other days she's in her office. Aside from the patients who are coming in for a quick follow-up visit, just about everyone who comes to her office is tense and upset, because she either has or thinks she may have breast cancer. Given that type of an environment, Sally's struggle to take downtime has been a recurring theme.

When she began her practice, she would schedule a day off or a vacation only to come into the office or do surgery anyway because a patient had an urgent need. "Almost every physician I have talked to about balance has had to discover his or her own limits by becoming totally depleted, which forced some changes," Sally says. "That is so difficult because the patient's need is real—she may be traumatized and stressed. It seems unfair to ask her to wait a day or two to come in or to see someone else; if I were in her shoes, I would want to talk to somebody today. The temptation is to drop everything and see that person because I care."

Sally has allowed herself to become exhausted many times because she didn't give herself the breaks she desperately needed. "I had to realize that even though taking a bike ride with a friend appears to be so much less important than helping a woman in crisis because she has breast cancer, it isn't," she says. "The truth is that I can't help my patients if I don't take care of myself. Sometimes I have to send that woman to another doctor who is in the office that day. I have had to learn that as much as I care, if I neglect my own needs for restoration and relaxation, ultimately both I and my patients lose."

Establishing such boundaries is humbling because it strikes at the heart of Sally's ego. "I have to acknowledge that I can't do it all, and God doesn't expect that," she says. "One thing that I have found helpful is accountability to others. Since I am single, that means staying in touch with a couple of close friends who know me well and with whom I am willing to be candid and vulnerable. Oftentimes they recognize before I do when I am getting overloaded and need a breather. I have learned to listen to their admonitions to take a break or make a change. I am increasingly convinced that we are poor judges of ourselves. We need others to reflect back to us truth that is perhaps more objective than our own analysis."

Sally tries to reserve Sunday as a day of rest. "For physicians, hospital rounds and calls may take up part of the day, but I guard the time that is available to really rest," she says. "I believe that's the way God intended it to be. I try not to let any kind of business encroach upon that. For instance, I love to tinker with the computer, and I occasionally write some programming for my office. But I don't let myself program on Sundays. I don't think that rest looks the same for everybody, but I do think it is a point of obedience to the Lord to decide ahead of time with him what the guidelines will be and then stick to them. For those working a full schedule on Sunday, another day of the week may be their Sabbath."

Sally finds refuge at her home, an uncluttered, simple abode in an older part of Dallas. She relaxes in the parklike setting in her backyard or plays worship music on her keyboard—her other favorite way to recharge her batteries. "In the evenings, I crave time with the Lord," she explains, "some time to sit down with the Word, to take my heart to him. I talk to the Lord as if he's a friend sitting by me in a chair. Some people see that as not being properly respectful, but that's how I relate to the Lord. And the music really ministers to me because it's a place of intimacy with the Lord. I could not be doing what I'm doing without those things."

These times of personal worship are particularly helpful when Sally is dealing with a medical situation that just doesn't seem fair. Several years ago, for example, a twenty-four-year-old woman who was seven months pregnant came to see her because she had a lump in her breast. Sally desperately hoped it was the type of benign tumor that commonly occurs with young women, but it was cancer. "As you can imagine, things like this situation touch my heart deeply," Sally says. "That's one time I just cried with the family."

This story had a happy ending: the woman had surgery while she was still pregnant, delivered the baby, underwent chemotherapy, and is fine today. But many other stories don't end as well. To cope, Sally has learned to take each case to the Lord. "What doesn't make sense I have learned to put in his hands, and I have realized I don't have to have answers," she says. "I don't know why tragedy occurs, but I do know that I can trust Jesus. His purposes and plans go well beyond this life and my understanding. Accepting that causes my roots to go down deeper in him. When I have stopped striving for an answer, I have found his peace surrounding me and comforting my heart. I know I can trust him, even in the face of unanswered questions.

"I don't know why Job suffered," Sally continues. "Everyone has a theory about it, and even after hearing many sermons on that subject, I still don't know why. What I do know is that we may pass through the valley of darkness, but God's intent is that we not camp there. We go through the valley, and then we climb the next mountain. When the journey involves the death of a loved one, I can't explain that. But somehow I don't have to because I know enough about God to be confident that he will in fact comfort, he will in fact redeem the situation, and all is not lost."

God at Work

Despite the pain, the trauma, and the pressure, Sally is in a unique position to see God at work in her patients' lives, often years after they have surgery for breast cancer. "God has taken that major stress and put it to good use in the patient's life," Sally says. "Perhaps the woman's priorities are different: maybe she takes more time out for her kids, or she's changed jobs to something she really enjoys, or she values every day. She calls her friends now when once she didn't have the time to do it. Many women have said to me, 'Breast cancer is the best thing that could have happened to me,' because they recovered and many positive things resulted in their lives. But that perspective comes only years later. If I were to predict such an outcome to a woman going through treatment, it would sound hollow and insensitive."

The advantage of being a follower of Christ in the medical field, Sally says, is the opportunity to realize the connection between positive changes in a patient's life and the work of God in that person's world. "If I wasn't walking with Christ, none of this would even dawn on me—I wouldn't see any of it," she admits.

Sally also is absolutely certain that without Christ in her heart, she would not be doing what she's doing today. "I wouldn't have had the wherewithal to apply for medical school, and I certainly wouldn't have had the courage to try a surgical residency," she says. "Even in my practice, he sustains me in a way nobody else can because he knows what the real need is. He's so creative, and it's so incredible to see his answers crop up when I least expect them."

3

Carmen Jones
MARKETING EXPERT

IT WAS THE SATURDAY AFTER THANKSGIVING in 1986. Carmen Jones and five of her friends were packed in her gold Hyundai, on their way home to Hampton, Virginia, after a long evening out. She was headed south on a newly constructed, poorly marked road when, reaching a spot where the traffic funneled into one lane, she lost control of her car.

As the car careened onto the soft shoulder and rolled over, Carmen was ejected from the driver's side window and thrown violently to the ground. It was like a bad dream—as she came to, she remembers thinking that it would be just a matter of moments before she would regain her composure and get to her feet.

It wasn't a bad dream.

When Carmen woke up, her roommate was standing over her, a panic-stricken look frozen on her face. She anxiously warned Carmen not to get up, and it was at that point that the twenty-year-old college junior realized she didn't have any sensation in her legs. All the other passengers had escaped serious injury, but she couldn't have gotten up if she tried.

As Carmen drifted in and out of consciousness, an ambulance transported her to one hospital, then a helicopter flew her to a larger one with a spinal-cord injury unit. As the doctor there began doing pinprick tests to determine what Carmen could feel, she slowly became aware that something was wrong. But she still thought it was only temporary.

"On a scale of one to ten," she asked the doctor, "what number would you give me to walk again?"

"One," he said.

"Then I knew this was serious," Carmen says today. "But I still remember thinking, *I'll show you.*"

That determination, though admirable, wasn't enough. The injuries Carmen sustained in the accident resulted in permanent paralysis from the waist down, leaving the five-foot, eleven-inch, fun-loving athlete confined to a wheelchair for the rest of her life. No more field hockey, no more basketball, no more running track: life as she knew it was over.

In the years since her accident, Carmen, now thirty-five, has come to see the tragic event as a necessary step in the unfolding of God's plan for her life and career. When she was confined to a hospital bed for six months, she never would have dreamed that she would one day speak on behalf of other disabled people at an antieuthanasia rally in front of the Supreme Court Building in Washington, D.C. Nor would she ever have imagined that she would one day start a business that helps large corporations market their goods and services to people with disabilities.

For one thing, Carmen ranked pretty low on the self-confidence scale before her accident. She's also African-American, a minority group that she says historically has not been very active in the disability movement. All things considered, she believes that she is the least likely person to do what she's doing. But God has an amazing way of using those very people to do the most significant things—a fact that Carmen simply cannot ignore. "I'm overwhelmed that the worst thing that happened in my life could become a launching pad for my career," she says.

Although Carmen was a believer before her accident, her relationship with Christ catapulted to a new level while she was recovering. "There's nothing like being on your back to make you cry out to the Lord for help," she says. "I am totally not the same person. My sister says I have had a heart transplant. Not that I was mean, but God has really reworked my inner being."

As a result, Carmen's approach to integrating faith and work has more to do with simply being herself than it does with trying to implement some kind of strategy or follow some carefully thought-out philosophy. After all, her career is intrinsically intertwined with who she is as a person, and who she is as a person is intrinsically intertwined with her faith in Jesus. She could no more separate the three than she could hop out of her wheelchair and run across the street.

"Jesus has rewired me from the inside," she explains. "Second Corinthians 5:17 says that if any man be in Christ, he is a new creation; the old has gone, the new has come! Those words have been fulfilled in my life. I now have a biblical world-view. God has been so gracious and loving to me that I have to realize my skill, joy, and life are demonstrations of his faithfulness. So if the opportunity presents itself for me to witness, to act with integrity, to provide an encouraging word, or to go against the grain and do the unpopular thing, I have to do it. Sure, there are moments when I am kind of hesitant to do or say certain things. But God wants to marry all aspects of our lives to who we are in Christ. People who aren't believers will say and do and be who they are, and he wants us to do the same."

One Step at a Time

These days, Carmen can say with confidence that the accident was the best thing that ever happened to her. But it took her a long time to reach that conclusion. She left the hospital after six months of difficult rehab, but a few years passed before she was able to work through all the issues that surfaced as a result of her injury. For example, she was mad at God. She didn't understand why other people going through rehab—people who didn't have a personal relationship with Jesus Christ—progressed faster than she did. She was frustrated because she had to put her college and career plans on hold, perhaps indefinitely. And she was grieving the loss of her mobility in much the same way a person grieves the loss of a loved one.

"There was a lot of denial," she admits. "It was probably two to three years before I was really settled and could feel comfortable about my condition. I just began to ask God to change my desire from walking to fully living life: 'If I'm going to live this life, you've got to show me how I can live it.' And he began to change my heart so that walking wasn't such a big deal."

Carmen left the hospital in May and returned to Hampton University in Virginia—in August. "Looking back, the amount of time that elapsed from the accident to the time I returned to school was very short," she says. "It was nothing but the Lord because I couldn't have thought of doing that on my own."

When Carmen began interviewing for jobs during her senior year, she had a hard time persuading anyone to hire her. At that time, employers weren't accustomed to dealing with job applicants in wheelchairs. On top of that, Hampton had never had a student with a disability looking for employment, so school placement personnel had no idea how to coach Carmen. "I had about thirty interviews my senior year, two second interviews, and no offers," she says. "I was very discouraged. I could not understand why these people didn't want to hire me. I felt very qualified and saw myself as a regular student competing for employment. It was unfathomable why anyone would be reticent or treat me differently."

Carmen eventually found work as a counselor at an independent living center in Hampton. She thought it was a good fit because although her degree was in marketing, she had at one point contemplated switching her major to counseling. In God's unfolding plan, however, it was a perfect placement because it helped her deal with some of those difficult issues relating to her disability. Less than three full years after her accident, she was helping people who had been disabled a lot longer than she to figure out how to become more independent. "While I was counseling my clients, I was counseling myself. I said, 'Oh God, you have a sense of humor!' It was a good experience because it helped me bridge the gap between who I was before the accident and my new status as a member of the disabled culture. Before then, I was never comfortable saying I was disabled or paraplegic."

After two years at the center, Carmen decided Hampton was too small. So she pulled up her stakes and moved to Washington, D.C., where she went to work for the U.S. Department of Transportation as a program manager in the Office of the Secretary. In 1992, she married Carlton Jones, a man she met and began dating after her accident. The following year, she transferred to the equal employment opportunity office at the U.S. Fish and Wildlife Service.

In 1995, after working for the federal government for four years, Carmen felt unfulfilled and dissatisfied with her job, so she went to work for Evan Kemp Associates. This multifaceted company sold medical equipment and independent living products, completed vehicle conversions for disabled customers, and also had a publishing/marketing arm. "We did a lot within that company," says Carmen, who served as vice president of marketing. "I was stretched and challenged with management issues for the first time, but it was exhilarating. The job at Evan Kemp Associates definitely shaped my confidence and my leadership ability. It developed me in so many ways, and I found that I couldn't wait to get up and go to work. That is the opposite of what I experienced with the government."

As Carmen worked on marketing programs with companies that manufactured products for disabled people, she began to realize that there was a disconnect between the disability community (which includes the firms that make products specifically for handicapped people) and the mainstream corporate community. The "aha" moment came one day when she was driving home from work, talking to her prayer partner on her cell phone. "I said, 'This is what I want to do: I want to help businesses develop marketing strategies that target people with disabilities.' And then it became a process of figuring out how to create the business that looks like that."

Carmen started her company, The Solutions Marketing Group, in 1998. She has worked with small manufacturers as well as nationally known corporations like Avis Rent A Car and America Online. Her largest client is American Express; she is working with a colleague to develop a strategic plan for the company to serve, market to, and employ people with disabilities across its four business units. That includes training existing employees to become more adequately equipped to serve the needs of the market, and developing a program that speaks specifically to the needs of people with disabilities. Carmen's role: "I am helping to create a credible message. A lot of times I find that companies think that they are including people with disabilities just by having someone roll by in a wheelchair in a commercial. That doesn't really do it. If you are going to extend the invitation, you have to have a staff that is well-trained to meet their needs. You have to be physically accessible. And you have to have an infrastructure in place so you can take care of this new consumer group."

"I Am Who I Am"

Back when Carmen was contemplating starting her own business, she told God that if he wanted her to do it, he would have to provide the clients. So securing the business of American Express helped her feel certain that she was on the right track. "God continues to confirm it for me because there are days when I feel like saying, 'Okay, forget it. I don't want to do this anymore,'" Carmen says. "And as soon as I go there, someone calls and says, 'We have this project' or 'We have this speaking opportunity and we'd like you to participate,' and it is exciting."

Carmen prays regularly that God will keep his hand on her business, but she knows she has to do her part too. That includes doing top-quality work, no matter what the cost. She refuses to compromise the quality of a project or product just to save a few pennies. She occasionally has had to absorb some expenses because she quoted a client one price for a marketing project and then had to add another element, such as a photo, that was more expensive. But if that's what it takes to provide a quality product and superior service, she's willing to do it. "We serve a God who has given us his best," Carmen says. "He does nothing half-heartedly, nor should we. I think that the secular world is looking for Christians to have something that is not up to par with what they have, so excellence is very important to me."

Keeping her word, especially when it comes to paying vendors on time, also is key for Carmen. That's not so much an issue these days when she's the one writing the checks, but it did come up at Evan Kemp Associates. Even then, she stood her ground. "I went to my boss and told him that he could withhold my salary in order to pay a vendor," she says. "That never happened, but he usually knew then how serious I was that this person get paid. That is how strongly I feel—if I tell someone something, then I have to follow through."

She's never been one to beat her coworkers over the head with the Bible, but Carmen has been in situations where she believes her faith has caused some spiritual warfare. When she was working for the government, for example, tension clearly existed between her and a colleague. "She thought I was getting opportunities that she wasn't getting, and she insinuated that I received this treatment because I was black and disabled,"

Carmen relates. "But I think it was deeper than that. One day, just in conversation, she said, 'You know, I'm an agnostic.' That, to me, said volumes. I thought, *That's why we're having tension.* Whatever part of Christ that was in me was making her very uncomfortable."

Carmen doesn't go out of her way to make people feel uncomfortable, of course. But she is not willing to change her behavior to fit a particular situation, however difficult it may be. "There's no undercover Carmen the Christian, and then Carmen the professional. I am who I am and people have to accept that."

As Carmen looks to the pages of Scripture for encouragement and for strength to remain true to who she is, she can relate to several biblical personalities, both in the struggles they faced and the situations in which God placed them. Take Esther, for example. "She had to make a plea to the king on behalf of the nation of Israel, and I feel, in a sense, that my work is like that," Carmen says. "I make a plea or a case to businesspeople about the disability market. So I am cognizant of whom I represent. I represent God, but I also represent other people with disabilities, and my behavior will make an impression on someone else. I have to be mindful of the people who come behind me."

Like Moses, Carmen has had to realize that God could use her despite her shortcomings and insecurities. "There are moments when I say, 'Lord, I can't do it. I can't go. I can't say what needs to be said.' And as he told Moses, God tells me that he will give me the words. I have seen a pattern in my life: I have often been placed in situations where I had no other choice but to rely upon God. Of course, I have to do my work; I have to prepare; I have to bring the skill set. But God has to gel all that together to make it work out."

These days, the story of Lazarus's death and resurrection holds special meaning for Carmen. When Jesus finally got to the scene and told the people to roll the stone away from the entrance to the tomb, Lazarus's sister Martha objected, "By this time there is a bad odor, for he has been there four days" (John 11:39). Jesus' response, in verse 40, is powerful: "Did I not tell you that if you believed, you would see the glory of God?"

Carmen says, "I was reading about Lazarus, and all of a sudden the words went *kerplunk* into my heart. It was as if God said to me, 'Carmen, you have to believe me and you'll see my glory. You can't do it in and of yourself.' That promise is one that I'm holding on to."

Taking a Stand

By nature, Carmen is a nurturer, sometimes almost to a fault. When she was working as a counselor at the independent living center, for example, a lady who suffered from intense migraine headaches came in for help. The woman couldn't function because she lived in a constant state of pain. As she talked to Carmen, her two children stood in the background, tears streaming down their faces because they were so hungry. This heartbreaking sight was more than Carmen could handle, so she began giving the family money. This may be an extreme example, but it clearly reveals a soft side that is an integral part of Carmen's personality.

But she also can be tough, particularly when it comes to standing up for what she knows is right. When she was with a previous employer, for example, Carmen found the language her boss used offensive: "It was sending chills up my back." She prayed about the situation, and then decided to talk to him about it. She actually went to his office to discuss another management issue, but during the course of the conversation she saw an opportunity. "I began to share with him that I was really uncomfortable with the words that he used, and I asked him not to use foul language around me anymore. His response was something like, 'Thank you for telling me. No one else would have had the guts to do that.' I think he had a puritanical view of me to a certain extent, but that was okay."

Some of Carmen's coworkers were into partying, even at official functions, and her conversation with her boss led him to begin looking to her to rein that in. "He didn't want the staff to damage the group's name," she says. "Not that I was a moral compass for the office, but he saw that my lifestyle lined up with the things that I was saying."

Carmen didn't just speak out about issues in private meetings with individuals, however. At one point, in fact, she felt compelled to take a vocal stand about a very touchy issue. A colleague in a leadership position was rumored to be having an affair with his secretary. The two had not been overt about their relationship, but one Friday evening at a special event that Carmen's department hosted, they threw caution to the wind. Their inappropriate behavior made it clear to everyone that they were, in fact, having an affair. Carmen refused to serve liquor at this event, but employees were allowed to bring their own alcohol, and this particular manager and one of his other employees got drunk. "I was really embarrassed because the more they drank, the stupider they acted, and the more the manager let his guard down about this relationship with his secretary," Carmen says.

Carmen was so disturbed by this behavior that she decided to bring it up at a staff meeting the following Monday. Twelve people—six senior managers and six middle managers—were at the meeting. Four of the twelve had been at the special event, including the two individuals who had gotten drunk. When her boss asked her what she thought of the special event, she let the group have it. "Before I get started, I have to share with you how disgusted I was by the conduct of the management staff that was there," she said bluntly.

Carmen didn't go into specifics about the indiscreet manager and the other employee who had gotten drunk. But everyone in the room knew how disappointed she was that these people had set a bad example and acted inappropriately in front of the rest of the staff, not to mention the outside guests who were at the event. "I was so mad, I was shaking," Carmen says today. "People were looking down and not giving me any eye contact. I believe it was a combination of shame and being caught."

The manager who was having the affair apologized to the group, but the harm had already been done. "It set into course the events for that woman's marriage to unravel, and it was awful," Carmen says. "That was probably one of the worst professional situations that I have ever encountered. I had to keep going forward while all of this was taking place, and that was such a challenge."

Joining God

In addition to taking a stand for what she believes in, Carmen has, throughout her career, looked for ways to share her faith in the workplace. When she worked for the government, she hosted a Bible study.

She has prayed with coworkers who have told her about a death in the family or some other difficult situation. She has sent inspirational cards to people going through tough times. "There's never a doubt about where I'm coming from," she says.

At the same time, Carmen has had to learn not to come on too strong. "We have all been around people who are real zealous believers, and that has turned people off," she notes. "When I was first discharged from the hospital, I was one of those people. When you saw me coming, you ran the opposite way."

Carmen's husband, Carlton, helped her reform her ways. "You want the Son to shine," he told her, "but you don't want to 'Son-burn' anyone."

Not all faith-sharing dilemmas have to do with speaking to coworkers about Christ's love, of course. As Carmen was developing the Internet site for the Solutions Marketing Group, she grappled with whether she should include links to Christ-centered sites on her home page. She bounced the idea off a couple of friends, who told her it was not the right time to do something like that. "The people I shared it with said, 'You are in a stage in your business where that doesn't do anything to enhance your site,'" she says. "That was something I struggled with: *If I don't make my Christian stand clear, am I diminishing my witness? Am I hiding? Am I cowering?* But I feel pretty comfortable that I'm not."

Carmen is a firm believer in the idea—articulated by Henry T. Blackaby and Claude V. King in *Experiencing God* (Broadman & Holman Publishers, 1998)—that God is always at work around us. In the same study, Blackaby and King also state that when God reveals to us what he is doing, that is our invitation to join him in his work. "He is doing whatever needs to be done to draw people to himself, so it's my job, I think, to partner with him to help that," Carmen says.

There have been times that Carmen has missed chances to speak about her faith; even though the door was wide open, she got cold feet. But she also is aware that her wheelchair affords her a unique opportunity to talk about spiritual things. Most of the people she works with are able-bodied, and many have never dealt with a person with a disability. So questions such as "How do you get dressed?" or "How do you drive?" are common. On subsequent meetings, the questions get deeper: "Carmen, why are you so happy?" "How can you handle being in a wheelchair?"

Carmen is careful not to be preachy when the doors open. If she knows a colleague well, she might say that Jesus Christ has taken care of her. Or if it's a developing relationship, she might just say that God gives her strength. She tries to be mindful of the fact that the people she's talking to most likely have preconceived notions about who God is and whether the Bible is true. But Carmen also knows that peace in the middle of difficult circumstances is a powerful testimony. "You cannot deny it," she says. "No matter where you fall on such questions as 'Did God really split the Red Sea?' you cannot deny a changed life and heart and joy in the midst of something that is so awful. And that is what God usually uses."

The Family Question

Carmen works out of her house. Unless she is visiting a client, her daily commute involves taking the elevator downstairs to the office in her Arlington, Virginia, home. She doesn't think she's prone to let work take over her life—she likes to have fun too much for that—but just in case, she has established boundaries to keep things in perspective. "Work time is a specific period during the day," she says. "But I don't do too well with rigidity. I realize work must get done, but I enjoy the latitude and flexibility of a home office."

That may change when Carmen has a family, of course—which brings up another subject she has had to leave in God's hands. For a long time after her accident, she told herself that she didn't want to have children, primarily because she was afraid of the toll that a pregnancy would take on her body. Now, however, after becoming pregnant and suffering a miscarriage, those fears have been replaced with a longing for a child. Happily, that longing soon will be fulfilled. Several months after her miscarriage, Carmen became pregnant again; she and her husband are expecting their first child in July 2001.

It took Carmen a while to formulate an opinion on life priorities and whether women should work professionally after they have children. She had to filter out everything she was hearing from other people and on family-oriented radio programs and concentrate on what she thought God was saying to her. But she finally arrived at the conclusion that God has a different plan for each woman, and it's up to that person to discern what the plan is. "I think God knows how I am wired and he is going to tell me what to do," she says. "I believe it is his design that the home be a Christian woman's priority. I realize that I may have to put plans on hold or scale back work schedules when children arrive. But what I had to change inside of me was my attitude. Before, I pursued my career at all costs. That is no longer the case."

For now, Carmen and Carlton have decided to hire someone to care for their child in their home during the hours when Carmen is working. "I am glad that I am formulating my opinion now rather than being blindsided by it," she says. "I don't want to sound as if I don't see the value of staying home, but I think God is big enough, and he provides enough flexibility and freedom, that if he is giving me a specific assignment in my work, I can discern how he wants me to balance all of the things in my life."

"Am I Really Here?"

In the meantime, Carmen is content to concentrate on her current role, one that often puts her in the most unlikely places doing the most unlikely things. For example, she's not exactly cyber-savvy, but last fall, she spoke at a conference called "Cyber Technology and the Information Age." Her eyes glaze over if a conversation turns to "HTML coding," but she was a perfect choice to address the conference attendees about marketing to people with disabilities. And when she was working for the Department of Transportation, she was asked to speak to a group about physical fitness. "I had to laugh! Who would have thought that I would be speaking to anybody about fitness? God does have a sense of humor!"

Maintaining her own sense of humor has been a key part of Carmen's ability to handle her disability, even when she was still trying to adjust to being a paraplegic. She began working for the independent living center right around the time that disability rights activists were lobbying for the passage of the Americans with Disabilities Act. During this time, she went to Washington, D.C., to lobby with other center staff members, and they ended up at a disability rights rally. What followed was a sort of out-of-body experience for Carmen. She remembers looking around, picking out the cool-looking wheelchairs and noticing all the various disabilities that were represented.

"I had kind of envisioned this whole disability community as being under this big 'We Are the World' banner, but it is not that way—it's very segmented," she says. "We were sitting there and this folk singer was singing this disability song—'We're disabled, and we're crippled, and we can't see'—and I was trying to control my laughter. It was just comical to me. I thought, *Am I really here? Am I supposed to be here?*"

Carmen may have wondered whether she was supposed to be at that particular rally, but several years later, when she was asked to speak at another rally in front of the Supreme Court Building, she knew it was the right place for her to be. It was a frigid January day in 1997, and the court was hearing arguments on a case about physician-assisted suicide. About five hundred disabled activists and five hundred other people gathered for the "Not Dead Yet" rally, which featured a keynote speech by former Surgeon General C. Everett Koop.

When the owner of Evan Kemp Associates had asked Carmen to speak at the rally four or five days before the event, her first reaction was, "Why me?" She didn't want to do it because she hadn't given the issue much thought, but spurred by Carlton's enthusiasm, she said yes. "I talked about the fact that because God has control of our lives, life and death are his decisions," Carmen says. "I was honored to have been invited to speak, and I was glad to share that viewpoint."

The five-minute speech garnered a good response from the shivering crowd, and it also continued to set Carmen on her course professionally. "It helped me to get over the anxiety of speaking, and it also helped me to see myself as more of a leader instead of just the worker bee," she says. "In the government, I was forced into a job description and a box. I saw myself as a supporting cast member, not as one who could develop policy or implement the program. So it was definitely a confidence builder."

During the last decade, Carmen has learned not to be surprised by anything that God brings her way, even if it thrusts her into the spotlight in Washington, D.C. And she can't help but be excited about the future of her career and her life.

"I am perfectly aware, specifically from my accident until now, that

God has been unfolding a plan," she says. "Sometimes I get impatient because his unfolding plan may be moving a bit slower than I'd like. What helps me to remain patient is that I know God is developing me into the person that he needs me to be for the work that he's called me to do. Since he's taken masterful care of me since I became disabled, I know that I can trust him to take care of the future. I remind myself daily that he's fully in control."

4

Bonnie Wurzbacher
FORTUNE 100 EXECUTIVE

IF BONNIE WURZBACHER COULD HAVE CREATED her dream job out of thin air, she couldn't have come up with a better fit.

In her previous sixteen years with the Coca-Cola Company, the forty-four-year-old executive had climbed the career ladder through seven positions, from regional account executive of the Minute Maid Company (a division of Coke) to vice president of business development for the U.S. fountain business. And while she'd had many challenging and interesting roles in her career, this latest opportunity—a promotion to vice president of customer strategy for the Coca-Cola Company—came out of the blue.

Though it was unexpected, Bonnie believed the move had God's hand all over it because her new role, which she assumed in October 2000, placed her squarely where her gifts and business interests intersect. She's passionate about starting initiatives and developing the infrastructures to support them, having done that several times throughout her career with Coca-Cola. The bulk of her success and experience with Coke had been in customer management, and she found international business one of the most interesting and challenging aspects of the company. And she had always wanted to work for the company's former president, a longtime Coca-Cola executive for whom she had great respect.

Looking back, Bonnie realizes that not getting a promotion she had hoped for earlier that year was the best thing that could have happened to her career. "While that was what I thought I wanted to do, God had different plans for me in a job that didn't even exist at the time," she says. "This has been another great lesson in trusting in God and learning to wait on his direction in my life. It just reinforced what I already know but sometimes have trouble doing, which is to pray for his will to be done in my life, not my will."

Every so often, Bonnie rewinds the tape of her professional life to look for ways in which God has intervened. Her latest promotion is a prime example. "You know he intervened when you clearly didn't make it happen, when what you thought you wanted was something very different, and events just unfolded," she explains. "I don't mean to sound like I attribute every tiny event that happens in my life to God, but there are so many more things than I often realize. You have to take the time to either see it when it's happening or to look back and see it, and this is one of those cases where I don't have to look too hard to see God's hand."

Over the years, this type of reflection has had an increasingly powerful impact on the way Bonnie lives out her faith at work. "I strive less and trust more because I've seen so many ways and times that God has directed my life and my career," she says. "The older I get, the more I realize how many things are out of my control. I've just learned to trust more and to be more patient as I wait for him."

Up the Ladder at Coke

Throughout her career, Bonnie has achieved success in many nontraditional roles for women. While quite a few talented, high-level women work at Coke, Bonnie helped women break new ground on the operations and line management side of the business. She has run one of the company's largest global customer teams. She has led the sales, marketing, and operations for a large part of the U.S. fountain business. And in most of her roles, she has been the woman in the most senior position and occasionally the only woman among her peers.

Hers is quite a list of accomplishments for anyone, let alone a former elementary schoolteacher who grew up in a family of ministers, teachers, missionaries, and doctors. Five years after Bonnie was born, her family moved from Chicago to Milwaukee, where her father pastored an independent Bible church for many years. Both of her parents and many other close relatives had gone to Wheaton College, a nondenominational

Christian liberal arts college in Wheaton, Illinois, so the idea that she might go somewhere else never really crossed her mind.

Growing up, Bonnie was always looking for ways to earn extra cash, either by selling things like lemonade and cookies or putting on magic shows, puppet plays, and other performances. But it never occurred to her that she had much of a business sense, or that finding ways to make money was something that naturally motivated her. So, given her love for children, Bonnie decided to follow in the footsteps of her mother and become a teacher.

But five years of molding the minds of second, third, and fourth graders was enough for Bonnie. She enjoyed teaching but found herself ultimately unfulfilled. She knew a number of businesspeople, though, and was intrigued by what they did, so she eventually decided to pursue a career in business. She thought she'd start by working for a publishing company selling curriculum to schools; instead she accepted a job with a small firm that represented food manufacturing companies. Two years later, in 1984, she went to work for the Minute Maid Company, a division of Coke.

Bonnie quickly discovered that the communication expertise, influencing skills, and ability to work independently that had served her well in teaching also were useful in sales. "I found myself to be a natural salesperson, if there is such a thing," she says. Bonnie's first big success with her new employer was convincing one of the company's largest soft-drink customers to start buying Minute Maid orange juice as well. This early accomplishment, snagging the company's first international juice customer, soon led to a corporate move to Houston, where Minute Maid was headquartered. Within six months, the business had grown so much that Bonnie began to work exclusively on that account. Then, in the summer of 1988, Coca-Cola secured all of that customer's U.S. juice business and Bonnie moved to Atlanta to be part of Coke's global customer account team.

By this time, she knew she was in business for the long haul, so she went back to school for more formal business training. Eighteen months later, Bonnie graduated from Emory University's executive MBA program. "I didn't have much of a life because I was working full-time, traveling internationally, and going to school full-time in a new place," she says. "Drive to Coke, to Emory, and to the airport: that's all I did for two years."

By the time she graduated, Bonnie was ready to try something new. She was chosen to build an organization and infrastructure to lead Coke's sales and marketing efforts with schools and universities in North America. This was the second new initiative that Bonnie led, and it gave her a crash course in the company's soft-drink business.

It was during Bonnie's three-year stint in this position that she met her husband, Steve, a senior executive in a related industry. They met while Steve was in Atlanta working on his company's Olympic planning. In a storybook sort of way, the couple fell in love at first sight and were married six months later, when Bonnie was thirty-seven.

The day the Wurzbachers returned from their honeymoon, Coca-Cola asked Bonnie to run the soft-drink business in North America for the large customer she had come to know so well early in her career. Three years later, in September 1996, she began running the southeastern region for the U.S. fountain division. In February 2000, Bonnie was appointed vice president of business development for Coca-Cola Fountain with responsibility for strategic planning, information systems, communications, and industry relations. And seven months later, she moved into her dream job.

As Bonnie reviews her career, she is a bit surprised at how far she's come, particularly because she's never considered herself to be the "corporate type." "I've ended up having the chance to do several entrepreneurial things within the context and with the resources of a large, successful company," she says. "What I've learned is that I can use my gifts and talents in many ways, and that is what God expects of me. Working for a great company gives me a real means of making a difference in my work on many levels, and I love that."

Integrating Faith and Work

Bonnie met Christ at a very early age, and the older she gets, the more she appreciates the heritage of faith that her parents and grandparents left her. "Growing up in a Christian family and going to Wheaton taught me very early on the importance of integrating your faith in your life," she says today. Her parents and many other adult role models—both at church and at college—taught Bonnie that faith in Christ is not confined to a Sunday worship service. "Your faith is just an integral part of who you are," she says. "You can't *not* integrate your faith and work because it's who you are. Just as you can't avoid integrating your faith and marriage. If you and your spouse are Christians, it is impossible to keep your faith separate from your marriage. It's how you approach your life."

Bonnie often turns to Scripture for instruction on blending faith and work, and she doesn't have to dig too deep for inspiration. "I go back to creation and Adam and Eve," she says. "God didn't just create them and plunk them in the garden to sit there. He said, 'I want you to have dominion over all that I've created.' People look at work as a curse from God, and I don't think that's it at all. I think that our God is a working God. Look at Jesus. He was here only thirty-three years in this world, and for many of them, he worked as a carpenter. Now why did he do that? I believe that God was a working God as a creator. Jesus was a working God as a human. There should be fulfillment in whatever your work is. It is the way we participate with God in his creation."

Bonnie is firmly convinced that God wants all followers of Christ to be his leaders, whoever and wherever they are. She believes this is particularly true for women. But women sometimes fail to put their God-given gifts and talents to use, either because they are focusing solely on raising their children, or because they are not encouraged to develop and use their talents and gifts in other ways. "I believe staying at home and raising children is a ton of work, and a great calling, and incredibly important," Bonnie says, "but I know people who have done beautiful jobs raising their children yet have no self-confidence outside that insular world. Are they using their gifts for God? I don't know. But I do know that God gave each of us talents that he expects us to use. And those gifts are so varied: not just business, of course, but art, music, teaching, counseling, and so many others. The guiding principle is that in whatever you do, work as unto God and not unto men [see Col. 3:23]."

But women don't necessarily have to seek outside employment to find an outlet for their gifts. Bonnie refers to a dear friend, the wife of an El Paso, Texas, attorney, who has raised five wonderful children but has never worked professionally outside the home. She does, however, lead a Bible study for about 200 women and another one for about 150 teenagers. "She's like a full-time minister without pay, and so between her terrific mothering and her ministries, I see her very much using her gifts and talents for good and for God," Bonnie says.

Bonnie doesn't have any children of her own, so she bases her perspectives about this subject on the experiences of her extended family and friends, as well as on her own personal study of Scripture. But a tragedy that struck her life a few years ago serves as a deeply personal reminder of how important it is never to jump to conclusions about businesswomen and their family situations.

In 1996, Bonnie happily became pregnant with identical twins. Inexplicably, she went into labor at twenty-one weeks. And although her tiny daughters were alive at birth, they lived only a few hours. Several miscarriages later, Bonnie and Steve have concluded that having more children doesn't appear to be part of God's plan for their marriage. So, trusting God in the absence of understanding, they are focusing on their relationships with the other children in their lives, including Steve's twenty-one-year-old son from his previous marriage and their many nieces and nephews.

Although Bonnie takes great comfort in God's promise that she and Steve will be with their little girls, Darby and Devyn, in heaven, it wasn't easy for her to give up her longtime desire to be a mother. Her experience with losing the twins and the other pregnancies has made her acutely aware of the fact that many people assume—incorrectly, she believes—that successful businesswomen simply choose not to marry and have children. Bonnie says, "I didn't plan to marry later in life; I just didn't find the person who was truly right for me until then. And I didn't choose not to have children. Many more women than men in business don't have children or aren't married, so often people jump to the conclusion that all these women care about are their careers. But I have found that rarely to be the case."

Over time, Bonnie has learned to look at her family situation more objectively. "It is very easy to allow yourself to think that someone else's life is better. But then you step back and look at all the blessings you have in your own life. My husband and I golf together twice a week; we travel;

we entertain often and share service projects—we do all kinds of things together that we couldn't if we had children. I still have my moments when I wish we had them, but mostly I'm so grateful I have other wonderful family and such a great life."

Bonnie doesn't broadcast the painful experiences she's had in life to everyone she meets. But she also doesn't shy away from talking about losing the twins if she thinks her story will encourage someone else going through a rough time. In fact, she looks at it as a way to do one of the most challenging tasks she faces as a believer in business: finding appropriate ways to share her faith with the people with whom she works. "I always feel that whatever crisis you've been through or will go through, you can't keep to yourself," she says. "People need to know they're not the only ones going through difficult times, whether it's at work or at home. And I really do believe that one of our responsibilities is to share our grief and how we've gotten through it with other people when they are facing similar circumstances.

"When you know you're God's child, you know that he is by your side through good and bad, and you know that one day you'll be with him and with those you love—that's what gets you through," Bonnie continues. "And being willing to talk about those hard times with people gets around to those truths eventually." (This belief led Bonnie to undergo training at her church to minister to members of the congregation who are in crisis.)

Bonnie takes advantage of natural opportunities to let people know that she's a follower of Christ both because she feels a biblical obligation to do so, and because she's found that it brings other believers out of the woodwork: "You can sometimes think, *No one else here is a Christian besides me,* but that's probably not true."

When Bonnie learns that a coworker is going through a difficult time, she goes out of her way to let that person know she is praying for him or her. She also doesn't hesitate to give her colleagues articles and books that have been particularly meaningful to her. "It's letting people know that you have a deep faith in God so that they'll listen for his still, small voice in God's perfect timing," she says. "Just knowing that there are others who trust their lives to God, in both the good times and the bad, can make all the difference."

Speaking the Truth in Love

In addition to discussing her faith as opportunities arise, Bonnie knows how important it is to reflect Christ whether she's in an executive committee meeting or giving instructions to an employee. "Trust me, it's not always easy, and I don't always succeed," she admits.

The process begins early in the morning. "If I don't start my day with prayer and meditation, I don't have the right mental approach," she says. "That's an important way to integrate your faith—by the way you think about your work. Your attitude and mind-set for the day impact the way you treat people and consequently, how they see you."

Ordering her mind before work helps Bonnie think clearly when she feels compelled to speak out about challenging issues. "I have always tried to seek and to speak the truth in a caring and loving way," she explains. "It's particularly hard to give negative feedback to an employee. A lot of managers are poor at it, so they just avoid it because they don't want to have to deal with the conflict."

The biblical concept of speaking the truth in love is a cornerstone of Bonnie's leadership style. In everyday work life, that could involve telling an employee the real reason why he didn't get a promotion or why she's being removed from a job. Or it could mean standing up for someone when others are groundlessly negative about him or her. For example, some years ago, Bonnie had a manager who had done a terrific job for her, but who later received poor performance reviews in a similar job from another executive.

Bonnie knew that what she was hearing didn't match her own experiences with the manager, so she decided to intervene on her behalf. It would have been far easier for Bonnie to think, *She's not my responsibility anymore,* and leave it at that. But in that case, she knew speaking the truth in love meant being willing to step forward and say, "That is not my experience; this does not hang together." Bonnie says, "I think you earn respect by consistently standing up for what is true and fair."

Of course, it takes courage to tell a boss that you believe he's wrong about something. It takes courage to tell people when their actions aren't matching their words. It takes courage to tell an employee the truth when she thinks she's doing a better job than she actually is, or when he thinks he should get a promotion when he really doesn't deserve it. "It's a lot easier to say, 'Oh well, there was just a better candidate' instead of 'There are three key areas where you just haven't performed. Here's what they are, and here's what you need to do to get to the next level,'" Bonnie says. "You have to be armed with the facts, and you have to be willing to deal with the conflict and the broken relationship that could occur. You hope that it won't, and if you do it in a caring way to a mature person, it won't."

As she deals with touchy situations, Bonnie admits she has to keep close tabs on her impatience that sometimes can flare into anger. "I have learned to try to calm down before I go talk with someone," she says. "I've learned to try to see things from other people's perspectives, to put myself in their shoes and think about the world as if I were in their job. That's been a hard thing for me to learn. But when anger is justified, I'm not afraid to show it."

Bonnie's husband has been helpful in her efforts to control her temper. "Steve is a great encourager, and he provides a sounding board and unconditional love," Bonnie says. "He also has a great sense of humor and a calm, thoughtful demeanor that is hopefully rubbing off on me!"

Bonnie also has learned to ask herself, *What would Jesus do?* when she is tempted to get angry. "While Jesus was known to express some justified anger, it was always much more justified than mine!" she says.

Balance in the Midst of Busyness

Throughout her career, Bonnie has spent anywhere from 25 to 75 percent of her time on the road, which leaves precious few hours for favorite hobbies such as golfing, cooking, and entertaining, not to mention spending time with family.

Discipline has been key to maintaining balance in her busy life. It was a lifesaver when Bonnie went back to school for her MBA. "I outsourced everything that wasn't that important to me, and I concentrated on what was. I had somebody else wash my car and clean my house so that I could focus on being with a friend or visiting my family or doing a service project. I had to cut out the rest."

Bonnie planned and she followed her plan. And it worked beautifully:

"I've never been more efficient in my life than when I was working, traveling, and attending school because I had to learn what to say no to."

Work is the same way, she believes. "You need to stay focused on what you're really good at, what the company is paying you to do, and what matters at the end of the year—not on the minutiae or the politics," she says. "This means you need to both prioritize and delegate. You need to say, 'Out of this whole list of things to do, these are the priorities. These I have to do, these I can delegate, and these I'm just not going to do.' Within the context of your world, you have to get good at that or you end up being ineffective at everything."

This is something that Bonnie has had to relearn with every new job. "A lot of managers got to where they are from doing everything themselves," she says. "And then they don't give their people the opportunity to develop because they're so busy directing and doing. I've had that problem at times. I've had to learn to give clarity on what success looks like and then get out of the way and coach my employees. I believe a coach doesn't tell you what to do; a coach helps his or her people figure out what to do and then provides tools, feedback, encouragement, and recognition."

Bonnie also has learned that hiring the best people is another way to facilitate balance in her life. "If you haven't surrounded yourself with great people, or if you've surrounded yourself with people who always agree with you—one of you isn't necessary," she says. "And if you're doing your people's jobs, you won't have any balance in your life, you just won't. The best managers I know hire capable people, let them do their work, give them the credit, and help them grow."

Bonnie takes her role as a coach and mentor—particularly to bright, energetic young women who are coming up the corporate ranks—very seriously. In fact, she believes that being able to influence and have an impact on others is the most rewarding aspect of being a woman in business. In addition to the people in her immediate organization, she often is mentoring two or three others at any given time.

Besides helping others to develop professionally, Bonnie says these relationships also give her a chance to demonstrate how her faith affects her life. "In a mentoring relationship, faith will often come up—it almost has to. You can't talk about life experiences in any deep way without it."

And faith leads to balance, which is an important lesson and legacy. "If the subject is comfortable for them, it certainly is for me," Bonnie says.

So what kinds of insights would Bonnie share with a young professional woman who was earnestly seeking to live out her faith at work? First, know yourself and be yourself. "When I say 'know yourself,' I'm talking about what motivates you, what you're good at, and what your gifts are," Bonnie explains. "The place where your passion and your skill intersect, that's where you want to go. It takes a while to figure that out. Then once you're there, be yourself because that's how you let your strengths out."

Second, always remember that God created you just as you are, and he loves you—no matter what others may think of you. "This gives you self-confidence. I don't see how you can have real success otherwise. God's already accepted you. Keeping that in mind—that you don't have to please anybody but him—is a freeing thing."

Third, be grateful for the good things about your life, your job, and your company. Bonnie says, "In any situation, it's just as easy to focus on the positive as it is to focus on the negative, and both are there. So be positive, be grateful, and have a good attitude. And if you can't do that, then do something that allows you to."

Fourth, learn from the bad times. "In one particularly difficult job situation, I learned a whole lot about what not to do," Bonnie says. "I learned how to be a better team player, how to give good, honest feedback, how to create an environment where people could thrive, how to coach people who weren't performing. I learned so much from that difficulty that I probably would do it again, just not for quite so long."

Fifth, you can't segregate your life, so don't try to live as if you can. "You won't find balance in your life unless you treat your life as a whole. You can't say, 'Okay, between the hours of 7 A.M. and 7 P.M., all I'll do is work, and from Friday night at six to Sunday night at ten, I will do only my family life.' You have to weave them in and make them work together."

Sixth, learn to use your gifts and talents for God wherever he puts you. Bonnie says, "I don't know if God cares if I work at Coke or somewhere else. What he cares about is that I serve him wherever I am."

Seventh, strive less and trust more. This last bit of advice is something Bonnie has learned to do as she's moved into positions of greater responsibility and visibility at the Coca-Cola Company. "You think from where you sit, you can figure it all out, and God certainly expects you to work hard and do your best and use your brain," she says. "But at the end of the day, you don't control very much. I could say, 'Well, I was well-educated, I took risks on jobs, I was willing to move, and I put in long hours,' and that's true. But I always remember what my minister, the late Dr. Frank Harrington, said so many times: 'If you want to make God laugh, just tell him your plans!'"

5

Joyce Godwin
GOVERNANCE EXPERT

THE YEAR WAS 1993, AND PRESBYTERIAN Healthcare Services in Albuquerque was looking to downsize. Executives wanted to avoid a layoff, so they began looking at other ways—job sharing, early retirement, and the like—to reduce the staff, which at that time numbered about six thousand employees.

As the statewide system's chief administrative officer, Joyce Godwin was actively involved with the restructuring process. As employees—a number of whom were Christians—contemplated their options, many sought her advice about what they should do. The whole situation had caused them to think about the possibility of doing something entirely new with their lives. Some considered going back to school to get a doctorate. Others contemplated becoming career missionaries or part-time missions workers.

As Joyce talked to these employees and prayed with them about their futures, she grew more and more excited about all the opportunities before them. That, in turn, led her to think about taking early retirement herself.

At first, the notion seemed impossible. After all, Joyce was the executive in charge of the whole downsizing effort, so she couldn't just leave in the middle of it. But the idea wouldn't go away. So later that year, at the ripe old age of fifty, Joyce cleaned out her office and said good-bye to the organization that had been her employer for more than two decades. She was ready for the next new thing that God had in store for her.

Joyce knew the timing was right for her to leave, but other people in the community, including some believers, didn't quite see it that way. Their misgivings were understandable; as she had moved into increasingly responsible positions with the health system, Joyce had become a role model for businesswomen in Albuquerque, especially businesswomen who were followers of Christ. "People thought I was abandoning them," Joyce says. "The Christians thought, *We have this Christian influence—now who's going to do that?*"

Joyce was sympathetic, but she also was confident that someone else would step up to the plate and provide the kind of Christ-centered leadership in the community for which she had become known. So, with the full support of her husband, Earl, she closed the book on that chapter of her life and moved on to the next one.

Although she officially "retired," Joyce didn't drop out of the marketplace, nor did she stop looking for ways to incorporate her faith into her work on a daily basis. Her positions as role model and spiritual influencer in the business world simply took a different—and much more global—form.

It was a form with which she was quite familiar.

In the mideighties, many corporations in New Mexico and elsewhere were adding women to their boards, and as a prominent woman in Albuquerque, Joyce was a prime candidate. "I was proven, I wasn't a rabble-rouser, and I wasn't a feminist, so I was a safe choice," she says.

Although her most prominent board role to date has been as a director of the Public Service Company of New Mexico, a $6.5-billion energy services firm, she has served on nearly a dozen other boards over the years. When she retired from the health system, she not only stepped up her corporate board involvement, she also continued serving on the boards of several major nonprofit organizations, including the Evangelical Council for Financial Accountability (ECFA), Mission Aviation Fellowship, and International Students, Inc.

As Joyce puts a microscope on her career, she clearly sees how God orchestrated events in such a way that prepared her perfectly for her role as a professional board member. From general manager of the San Jose Chamber of Commerce to vice president of diversification with Presbyterian Healthcare Services, each position gave her a chance to hone different skills and develop areas of expertise that she now draws upon in her board work. Board governance is the number one concern that surfaces when the ECFA conducts field reviews with its nearly one thousand member organizations. And as a governance expert who also happens to be the chair of the ECFA board, Joyce is uniquely positioned to influence the way those organizations do business.

"Governance is not an end of itself," she says. "It exists to facilitate doing ministry. But if the governance is not done right, the whole ministry could be destroyed. So much of my career has been in support functions; for example, with healthcare, I wasn't doing the surgery, but I did the behind-the-scenes work to facilitate other people doing it: preparing them, encouraging them, and facilitating their doing the very best job they possibly could. That's transferable to governance—you want excellence there so that the governance doesn't become a stumbling block to the work of the ministry."

Laying the Groundwork

Now nearly fifty-eight, Joyce has no plans to stop working, although her current schedule permits her and her husband, a semiretired anesthesiologist, to indulge in one of their favorite pastimes—traveling. At last count, they had been to more than eighty-three countries—from Antarctica to Zaire (now Democratic Republic of Congo) and many points between—both for vacations and short-term mission projects. Many of the latter trips have been to missionary hospitals. While her husband teaches anesthesia to local staff members, Joyce does everything from clerical work to organizing medical supply shelves. And every now and then, she is asked to tackle a larger assignment. At a hospital in Africa, for example, she interviewed the department heads about their problems and concerns, and then used that information to write a paper about how to move the hospital from being missionary-run to being managed and "owned" by the experienced Africans. Although that was about fifteen years ago, Joyce still gets reports from the hospital staff about the progress they are making, she says.

When she's not traversing the world, Joyce often can be spotted hopping from airport to airport, from one board meeting to the next, throughout the United States. She does this without losing her sanity, or her luggage, for one simple reason: she is one of the most organized people on the planet. That may seem like an overstatement, but Joyce has a remarkable ability to juggle numerous tasks and responsibilities, and to do them all well. She doesn't spend her days racing to mark items off her to-do list with all the flexibility of a drill sergeant. She just knows exactly what she has to do, when she has to do it, and how long she has to get it done.

Take, for example, her finely tuned approach to air travel. Whenever possible, she tries to book her domestic flights on Southwest Airlines. That's not just because the employees are friendly and seem to love what they do, although that does appeal to her. It's primarily because she knows that if she gets to the Southwest desk an hour before takeoff, she can be in the first boarding group, which means she can get on the plane earlier and have her pick of the seats. No rushing around, frantically trying to catch a flight at the last minute, no stumbling over fifty other passengers in search of an empty overhead compartment. She does it all in an orderly and organized manner, which greatly reduces the stress that can accompany the accumulation of many thousands of frequent flyer miles each year.

Joyce didn't suddenly become organized when she became an adult, however. Her ability to get things done has served her well since childhood.

Born in Washington, D.C., in 1943, Joyce began working at a very early age. When she was seven, she sent away for a sales kit and began selling Christmas cards door-to-door. The card company probably would have been shocked to learn that it was encouraging the career of a second grader, but Joyce did very well with her little business. Holiday card sales were lucrative in October and November, but Joyce quickly realized that if she wanted to make the most of her growing customer base, she'd need to expand her product line to include assorted greeting cards for year-round use. At her age, she had no understanding of such business terminology, but her entrepreneurial bent was obvious.

Joyce's family moved to Miami when she was about thirteen, and she quickly obtained a waiver so she could work at that age. She spent the next summer doing clerical work in the medical records department of a local hospital. After that, she spent the next four summers at a veterans hospital in Miami, collecting clerical experience in the personnel, purchasing, and research departments.

"Looking back, I can see how all of that was orchestrated because those were all areas that later in life I supervised," Joyce says. "My own supervisors let me do a lot more than what I was hired to because they saw I had initiative and I could get things done. When I look back on it, I can see I was doing much more than they were paying me for! I was cheap labor, but it was a great learning experience."

In addition to working at the hospital during the day, Joyce worked various night jobs in the summer so she wouldn't have to hold multiple jobs during the school year. That job-juggling experience taught her the time-management skills that she so deftly uses to organize her life today. And by saving money she earned from the jobs she held from elementary through graduate school, she was able to pay for her tuition and other college expenses, plus help out with her family's finances.

Neither of Joyce's parents graduated from high school, nor did they have particularly high career aspirations for their daughter. They saw that Joyce was good with numbers, so they would have been pleased if she had decided to become a bank teller after high school. But most of her friends were college bound, and she went to college because it seemed like the thing to do.

When Joyce enrolled at Florida State University in 1961, her faculty adviser, an older woman, told her she had two options: she could pursue either nursing or teaching. Neither was appealing to Joyce; if she had been able to take a skills assessment test, she might have majored in business or accounting. But such tests weren't available, so she wound up with a degree in government. She went on to earn a master's degree in political science and public administration at George Washington University in Washington, D.C.

She met Earl in graduate school. After marrying in 1967, the couple moved a few times—first to San Jose where Earl completed his residency, and then to Corpus Christi where he served as a navy doctor for two years. By virtue of her after-school and summer employment stints, Joyce had put together an impressive résumé by the time she entered the work force officially after college. It grew more impressive as her career progressed; by the time Joyce went to work for Presbyterian

Healthcare Services in 1973, she had experience in lobbying, public affairs, finance, and management with a large chamber of commerce, she had served as director of staff development with a hospital in Texas, and she had taught political science at a university in San Jose, among other things.

Along the way, Joyce achieved many "firsts" for a woman. She established this pattern in college when she was the first female to be elected vice president of the student body at Florida State University. Later, she was the first woman to serve as chairman of the Greater Albuquerque Chamber of Commerce, the first to head a United Way campaign in Albuquerque, and on a broader scope, the first female to serve as chairman of ECFA, Air Serv International, Mission Aviation Fellowship, and International Students, Inc. "To me, being the first woman was not an important thing, but it has been important to other people," she says.

Joyce never really set out to get any of these positions; she just made the most of the opportunities she had. In the early years of her career, it didn't even cross her mind that God was guiding her path. "In one way, you could look at it as I was kind of drifting along, going with the flow," she says. "Or when you look at what I've done, you might think, *Oh, you were planning for that.* But I have to say now that it was all the Lord's timing. He was opening doors and if not pushing, certainly nudging me through them."

Primary Influencers

Joyce had gone to church most of her life—she had, in fact, received the Outstanding Religious Leadership award in college. But although she was active in church, she had no concept of what it meant to know Jesus Christ personally until she and Earl began attending a small Presbyterian church in Albuquerque. "We knew there was something different about it, but we didn't know what," she says.

The Godwins got involved with the church's "inquirer's" group, and it was there that they first understood how God calls people to have a personal relationship with him. "The group examined questions such as 'Who is Christ?' and 'Who is the Holy Spirit?'" Joyce says. "Working through all these, it came together in a big way."

By this time, thirty-year-old Joyce had begun working for Presbyterian Healthcare, initially as director of education. In that role, she spent a lot of time interviewing key staff members within the system about the educational needs of the employees, from GEDs for people who had never finished high school to leadership training for the medical staff. At the top of her list of interviewees was Marion Kellogg Van Devanter, who had begun working for Presbyterian in the twenties when it was a sanatorium for tuberculosis patients. Marion, whom everyone affectionately called "Mrs. Van," was the heart and soul of the health system. But the only thing Joyce knew about her at that time was that everyone she met seemed to think Mrs. Van walked on water. "I was kind of rolling my eyes during all of this, thinking, *Nobody is that good*," Joyce admits.

One day, Joyce went to visit Mrs. Van at her little house by Presbyterian Healthcare's largest hospital. "She looked at me and said, 'You're finally here. I've been praying about you coming,'" Joyce says. "It was as if she had been given a visual image of what I was going to look like. Later I thought, *Oh my goodness*, but at the time, I took it in and thought, *This woman is unbelievable*."

Joyce, who was still in the early stages of her own spiritual development, felt an instant closeness to Mrs. Van. In addition to becoming a spiritual mentor to Joyce, Mrs. Van also showed the younger woman how to incorporate her faith into her work. "She had gifts of encouragement and mercy and giving—she was just modeling her faith every day," Joyce says. "When she couldn't walk outside because her eyesight was so bad, she walked around her house to get her exercise, quoting Scripture the whole time or praying, particularly when she had concerns about something. She laid all of it on the Lord, and I was really taken with that."

By watching Mrs. Van, Joyce could see that a person didn't have to have the spiritual gift of evangelism to be able to share her faith with others. St. Francis of Assisi's oft-quoted line—"Preach the gospel every day; use words when necessary"—applied as well to Mrs. Van as it did to Mother Teresa, Joyce says. "Even though Mother Teresa made her faith very clear, she didn't have to do that—people knew. They could see Jesus in her. I think that's how people saw Mrs. Van; they would look at her and say, 'That's Jesus.'"

The desire to apply biblical principles to everyday work activities was a natural outgrowth of Joyce's relationship with her beloved mentor. "I could see how Mrs. Van did it, so I had a great model. From the time I became a really strong believer with a personal relationship with Christ, I don't think I ever segmented my life—'here is church; here is work; here are friends.' It was integrated from the beginning."

As Joyce thinks about biblical characters who have inspired her in this integration process, she frequently is drawn to the life of David. "What attracts me about him is the integrity of his heart for God," she says. "He was not some perfect being, but he was a strong leader, and he was so prepared through all the stages of his life."

Because David had a heart for God, he also was patient and willing to wait for God's timing. That's something to which Joyce can relate. She doesn't think she's been particularly ambitious in her career; she's simply taken opportunities as they opened up to her. On the other hand, if she had been driven to reach a certain position or achieve a certain title, she thinks plenty of people would have tried to block her. "If I had said, 'I've got to be in this job by this time,' or 'I covet being chairman of this ministry,' people may have thought, *Who does she think she is?*" Joyce says. "Instead, by not being ambitious and just being available and prepared, when I took a new opportunity people could celebrate with me."

Guided by Faith

Throughout her career, Joyce's faith has been the foundation upon which she has based her work. It also has been her strength in the midst of difficult and challenging circumstances, such as when she joined the board of the Public Service Company of New Mexico (PNM). Prior to becoming a director in 1989, she had gone to a couple of board meetings as a guest, and at those meetings, talk of mergers and acquisitions in the energy industry made her feel as if she was in way over her head.

She had no idea.

At her first official meeting as a member of the board, Joyce learned that a number of shareholder class-action and derivative suits had been filed against the company. The suits challenged key decisions PNM officials had made over a twenty-year period, with emphasis on the company's diversification efforts. Joyce was the only director not named as a defendant in the suits because she had not been on the board when the events that were at the heart of the investigation took place. As a result, she was the sole member of a special litigation committee that had to investigate the other directors.

Not only was Joyce the only woman on the nine-member board, she also was twenty years younger than most of the other directors. So her first job as a board member was daunting, to say the least. "They must have seen me as a little kid, and I was a woman to boot," she says today.

Joyce went into the investigation thinking that the likely result would be a report that showed some things could have been done differently but that nothing unethical or illegal had taken place. She couldn't have been more mistaken.

The study took 2,100 hours of her time, with the attorney fees over the three-year period totaling $23 million. After the completion of the special litigation committee's work, a new CEO and a completely new board—with the exception of Joyce—were appointed. "This was big-time stuff," Joyce says. "The litigation was making the headlines in the paper all the time."

Early on, she searched the Scriptures for guidance. "I wrote down a number of verses that pertained to my situation, and I put those in my calendar so I could constantly refer to them before I went into each session," she said. Philippians 4:6—"Do not be anxious about anything, but in everything, by prayer and petition, with thanksgiving, present your requests to God"—was particularly encouraging to Joyce during the investigation.

While Joyce had selected expert advisers and legal counsel to work with her in the investigation, she knew she also needed spiritual help. "I made a list of my friends whom I saw as real prayer warriors, and I enlisted them as a support system," she says. She couldn't go into too much detail about what she was doing, of course, but she desperately needed her friends to pray for her while she conducted the business of the investigation. "Talk about circumstances," she marvels. "I wasn't chosen for the board with this in mind, but all these lawsuits came, and I was the only noninvolved person on the board. So I figured I was supposed to be doing that job. But I felt others should be praying for what needed to happen. That was just wonderfully reassuring to me. I could go into those interview sessions with confidence because people were supporting me by praying for me."

Another Type of Stewardship

When Joyce was growing up, her family never had much in the way of material possessions, but she was too busy earning money for her own basic needs to worry about coveting other people's things. Even as adults, with plenty of financial resources at their disposal, she and her husband have shied away from accumulating too much "stuff." They've lived in the same house since 1973, and they have no interest in a new or second home.

The fact that Joyce and her husband have always lived beneath their means has given them an added measure of flexibility. "When we both retired when we were in our fifties, people asked, 'How can you do that?' Well, we weren't out buying new houses; we didn't have a beach house or a cabin," she says. "And we have no desire for those things. We'd rather invest in short-term missions and ministry work."

Such talk of financial responsibility brings up another principle that has guided Joyce through the years. She has always believed that it's important to be able to walk away from a job if, after taking a clear ethical stand, she doesn't see a difficult situation change for the better. "To me, that's always been a very freeing thought," she says. "I think a really bad position to be in would be feeling you have to keep a job or you have to keep a position, especially when you're in a job that pays a lot of money. If you don't feel that you could leave at any time, that's when you could have problems with ethics and integrity. You could start compromising, justifying little things. You might say, 'Okay, I'll give on that point because it's not a huge issue, and it's more important that I stay here as a Christian woman. I can have a bigger impact later.' But then how about the next point?"

Financial carelessness invites such compromise, Joyce believes. If a person has a huge house payment and a couple of large car payments, it's difficult to leave a well-paying job, no matter what the ethical underpinnings. She describes the dilemma this way: "For an ethical decision, are you willing to sell your house and move to a smaller place if you don't have the money coming in? If it's a situation where your employer is going to make it hard for you to get another job because you're leaving on some ethical principle, do you want to continue working there anyway?"

Modeling Balance

Fortunately, Joyce has never been in a position where she actually had to leave a job because of an ethical problem. And although she readily admits that there were many years when she worked entirely too much (sixty or seventy hours a week), she never felt work was consuming her life. "When I was working so hard, I didn't consider myself a workaholic," she explains. "I enjoyed what I was doing, and because I didn't have things compartmentalized, I was seeing it as a ministry. I was getting to have a positive impact on people's lives."

That ministry continues today. Joyce is a natural encourager and mentor, and she spends a good deal of time sending inspiring notes and birthday cards to the people she's come to know over the years.

The Godwins don't have children, so Joyce hasn't had to deal with the stress of juggling work and family to the same extent that a working mother would. But she still has had to be intentional about maintaining balance in her life—a task made infinitely easier by her ability to stay organized. "To me, out of structure comes freedom," she says. "So if part of my life is structured, then I have great freedom to do other things. And to be structured, I have to be organized. I figure out in advance what I have to do in order to get to a certain point, so then I can be spontaneous, and I don't get into the habit of working all the time because I've planned not to work all the time. There's not a last-minute crisis of 'This is due tomorrow'—it's all planned."

Joyce serves on nine boards concurrently. As if that weren't enough to keep her busy, for several years, she has served as chairman of as many as four ministry boards at one time. The role of chairman requires a significant time commitment; in addition to attending regular board meetings, she serves as a mentor and adviser to the CEO of each organization, she conducts the CEO's performance evaluation, and she stays in regular contact with the other board members between meetings.

Many of those board meetings are clustered in the spring and fall, which could be a logistical nightmare for Joyce were it not for her penchant for structure. "I help set the meeting dates," she says. "If I make sure that everybody sets meetings a year or two years in advance, then it's not hard to manage."

When Joyce was working full-time, one of the ways she modeled balance for her employees was by carefully scheduling her vacations each year. "Some of this was forced by my husband's anesthesiology group—they did their vacation planning every August for the next calendar year, so I needed to make plans in advance."

Joyce's unusual habit of taking three-week vacations raised some eyebrows because some of her colleagues didn't think being away for that long was compatible with the work she was doing. But she did it anyway. "I modeled that you could take three weeks—you could do just fine if you were organized," she says. "And it probably was better for the other employees that I was gone for that long because they could become stronger and less dependent.

"If somebody has a serious health problem and he or she is out of the office for three, four, or six weeks, people adjust and learn to handle things. Perhaps if we took more time taking care of ourselves and planning time away, we'd have fewer stress-related illnesses and a fresher perspective when we returned to work."

Once, Joyce even took some vacation days in the midst of crisis at work. "I said, 'I could stay here now but maybe in two weeks there's going to be another crisis, and I'll need to be there for that one,'" she says. "People respected enough of what I was doing that they didn't say, 'You can't do that.' But in some ways, it showed them some balance—that time with Earl was important, and I was going to have it."

That's not the only way Joyce demonstrated balance, however. During her last few years at Presbyterian Healthcare, she hosted a Bible study at noon every Thursday in her office. "That was important because I was giving up 20 percent of my lunches each week, and those were always business lunches," she says. "Again, some people questioned it by saying, 'How can you do that? You need to use every one of your lunches to be out doing something.' But they saw that I was faithful—that that was sacred time. They saw the women coming in with their lunches and Bibles every Thursday. So I feel it was real modeling."

Joyce doesn't have to worry about daily business lunches anymore, but in the midst of her busy schedule, she's still committed to planning downtime. For example, for the last several years, she has made a point of scheduling a "day with the Lord" each month. "I'm a good scheduler, and if I have it marked out, I'm quite good at telling people, 'No, I'm not available to do that, I've got an all-day commitment,'" she says.

There's no set agenda for those special days. Joyce might spend the day at home reading Scripture, or she might spend it in a park, reading inspirational books. God seems to bless her commitment: "On those days, if I'm home, I don't get phone calls, and usually my phone is ringing all the time. Faxes aren't coming in that I feel I have to do something about right away. It's as if God says, 'She needs quiet time to do this.'"

Although Joyce's monthly day with the Lord is important, it is no substitute for her daily devotional time. She believes that being right with God is the key to blending faith and work, whether that work is a full-time job as a senior executive of a healthcare system or a volunteer role on the board of a nonprofit organization. And the only way to maintain that right relationship is through time and communication. Whether Joyce's quiet time is first thing in the morning, after breakfast, or later in the day isn't the issue; what matters is that she has a quality time of prayer and Bible study each and every day.

"Certainly, when I would feel that I wasn't living out my faith at work, it would be because I wasn't spending time with the Lord," she confesses. "It's hard to live out your faith when that relationship is not growing and it's not the center of attention for what you're doing."

6

Susie Case

PROFESSIONAL VOLUNTEER

EVEN AS A YOUNG CHILD, SUSIE CASE had a passion for helping women improve themselves.

When she was a preschooler, she would line up her dolls and tell them what they needed to know to make their lives better. After all, if she knew how to tie her shoes, they should know how too. As a third grader, she once gave her teacher advice on how to teach poetry writing. "Mrs. Chamberlain," she said, "if we write poems to the melodies of songs that we know, it might help the kids who are having problems figuring out how to make their poems rhyme." And as a sophomore in high school, Susie told her French teacher (who, incidentally, was from France) how she could grade her tests to make her corrections easier to understand.

Although young Susie might have come across as a little know-it-all, she was sincere in her efforts. She had, and still has, a strong need to take truth and show people how to apply it for their own self-improvement. Now, however, she no longer has to address make-believe audiences or tell her superiors what to do. Instead, this forty-three-year-old former equity analyst is putting her wiring to good use in her role as teacher of a Bible Study Fellowship (BSF) day class in New York City, a position she's held since 1992.

When Susie isn't handling BSF business—she devotes about twenty-five hours a week to lesson preparation, leadership training, and teaching for this intensive thirty-two-week class—she is busy running her home, a spacious apartment on Manhattan's Upper West Side. This enterprise includes taking care of husband Bob, an investment banking executive with Salomon Smith Barney, and their two children, twelve-year-old Carl and eight-year-old Sarah.

Her life today is a far cry from what it was fourteen years ago, when Susie was headed up the corporate ladder on Wall Street. But she's confident that the choices she has made, though sometimes difficult and often tough on her ego, have been the right ones for her and for her family. "When I first stayed home, I had no idea whether the kids would really benefit from it," she says. "The Bible said to train up children in the way they should go, and I thought, *Well, there isn't a Christian school nearby, so I guess that means me.* But now, when I get feedback from people about my children's kindness or their obedient spirit or their willingness not to take the limelight, I say, 'Wow—it works! God's way actually works!'"

Setting the Stage

Susie's father used to say that wherever she was, the action was. Always upbeat, she's also thorough, energetic, and bouncy (earning her the childhood nickname of Wiggle Wart). "When I worked full-time, I often sat on top of my desk cross-legged because it was painful to sit in a chair—I don't like sitting still at all," she says. "So I love being home. It was prison for me to go to a little office and try to stay there, but now that I am basically running a business called the Case Family, I never sit still. I don't have that option."

Susie loves books and she will read "anything, anytime," especially self-help books and biographies. As a child growing up in Pasadena, California, she also enjoyed writing and might have pursued some sort of literary degree if her father hadn't convinced her otherwise. "He said that women English majors were a dime a dozen. I had strong math scores, and he said if I majored in something related to math, the world would be my oyster."

To a great extent, he was right.

Susie went east to college, earning a degree in applied math from Harvard University in 1979. After working for a few years, she returned to Harvard, this time for an MBA. "My dad and my uncle both went to

Harvard Business School, and my mother completed a one-year program there," she explains. "That was just what the Petersons did. I really didn't ever think about whether it was something I wanted to do."

Her undergraduate studies included an emphasis on rudimentary computer science, and it was this background that propelled her into the spotlight after she finished business school in 1983. She went to New York, where she got a job on Wall Street as a stock analyst following technology companies. Her career progress also was spurred by the fact that she had a boss who believed it was important to play people against type. He had men covering cosmetic companies and women covering waste-management firms; "I was particularly pleasing to them because I was a perky little brunette who could talk technology," Susie says.

Susie had grown up in a culturally Protestant home—her parents went to church but were not professing believers. She had begun to feel the need to know if God was real a few years after finishing business school, but it wasn't until November 29, 1987, that she understood what it meant to accept Christ personally.

A friend from work took her to a Campus Crusade for Christ outreach dinner for executives that featured a joint testimony by Don Hodel (secretary of the interior and secretary of energy under President Reagan) and his wife. As the Hodels spoke candidly about how their son hung himself when he was in high school, their story struck a chord deep within Susie. Only a few years earlier, her own alcoholic mother had drunk herself into a coma—probably deliberately—and died. Susie was amazed that the Hodels, who appeared so outwardly successful, had baggage. And not only that, they were willing to stand up and talk about it. "I had never talked about my mother drinking, much less the fact that she actually drank herself to death," Susie says.

Susie accepted Christ that night, and by Friday of the same week, she knew her life was different. Incidentally, the Hodels' speech didn't do a thing for her then-fiancé, Bob. The two married in 1988, but Bob didn't become a believer until 1990. His conversion also occurred at a Campus Crusade outreach dinner. This time, however, the speaker was former U.S. Senator Bill Armstrong, who testified that he had it all but woke up one day and said, "This isn't enough." He discovered Christ in his quest to find out what else was out there. "Bob said, 'That makes sense to me,' and accepted Christ," Susie says. "It was an act of grace by God that he had us end up equally yoked."

A New Career

Nine months and three weeks after Susie and Bob got married, their son was born. While she was pregnant, Susie had every intention of going back to work after the baby came. She wanted to buy a studio apartment in her building for a nanny who would care for the baby when Susie was on the road (at the time, she was traveling two hundred days a year). But late in her pregnancy, en route to East Lansing, Michigan, from Chicago, she changed her mind. She was reading the Bible, and she heard God's voice—"In the way that Christians know that it is God's voice"—telling her to stay home. "It was almost as if I were a third person looking at the situation, saying, 'Stay home? That doesn't make any sense,'" Susie says. "But I knew it was what I was supposed to do."

Susie was a relatively new believer. She didn't know the Bible well yet. She didn't have a group of friends who shared her faith. Both of her parents had died, so she didn't even have a close relative to tell her what to do. She was on her own: "I think God gave me a particularly strong prompting from the Spirit because he says he takes care of widows and orphans, and he was taking care of me."

When Susie told her boss that she was quitting, his reaction was totally unexpected. "He told me, 'If you were my wife, that is what I would want you to do,'" she says. "It was an incredible confirmation." She was a bit more reluctant to tell Bob, in part because she thought he had fallen in love with her because she had her own life and would, therefore, be "low-maintenance." His response? "I knew you would get there."

"It was what he wanted, but he wasn't going to tell me," Susie says. "You aren't supposed to encourage women to give up their dreams."

The fact that the two most important men in Susie's life agreed that her staying home was the best thing for her to do made the decision easier. But actually leaving the workplace—she worked full-time until a week before Carl was born—was "hugely hard."

"I am a verbal person," Susie says. "I was in a job where I was paid to make phone calls and visit people, and then I was staying home in an apartment with a preverbal baby."

At that point, Susie decided she wanted to leave New York City. But Bob didn't want to commute. "So I spent four years trying to find the right situation to entice him out of the city. Four-and-a-half years into it, I realized that when he said he wasn't leaving, he really meant he wasn't leaving."

Although Susie would readily admit that she leads a privileged life, she also can relate to the sacrifices made by her biblical role models Moses and Paul. In BSF, she spent a year studying the life of Moses and another year studying the Book of Romans, so she is well acquainted with the challenges these men faced. "Both of them struggled enormously with wanting a different ministry than the one the Lord gave them," she says. Moses, for example, was resentful that his brother and sister had grown up in their parents' home. Because he had grown up in the pharaoh's palace, he never fully fit in with the Jews, but he was still called to lead them. And Paul, though he was asked to evangelize the gentiles, continued visiting the temple (even though the Scriptures don't say that God specifically told him to do that) because he wanted to share the gospel with the Jewish people.

"In both of their cases, they were leaders for whom the very act of leading was a daily sacrifice because it wasn't where they wanted to be. But it didn't matter, because that's what God asked them to do," Susie says. "This didn't apply so much when I worked in the marketplace, but it applies now. It will always be a struggle for me to be out of the limelight. And it is tough to be a stay-at-home mom in a city of professional go-getters. But once I had children, I really felt that God asked me to raise them, and New York City is where he's asked me to do it."

Household Manager

Susie sometimes thinks about going back to work, but her family certainly has enjoyed having her home. "If you have an MBA running your household, that is a pretty high-level hire for the job," she says, smiling. "They love the fact that there are all these nuances in our household that happen because I attack it with my full energy."

For example, Susie is constantly thinking about "flow" in her home. In 1906, when her building was built, fine Victorian women never stepped foot in their kitchens. Foreign maids did all the cooking and served the meals in the dining room. But times have changed. So Susie recently undertook a remodeling project that will let her children spread out their work in the kitchen while she cooks. "I know Bob appreciates that I'm always thinking, *What can we do to make this as excellent as possible? What can we do to make the schedule excellent, to make the home excellent?*"

One of the ways Susie lives out her faith as manager of her household is by abiding by the biblical principle of submitting to her husband's will when, after discussing a household issue, they still don't agree. Some people say Scripture passages on submission apply only to the culture of New Testament times, and others say wives should submit with blind obedience. Susie, however, believes that submission still applies to our time, as long as it is with thoughtfulness. "Generally, Bob supports my management decisions, but there have been occasions when he asked me to do something I disagreed with," she says. "When I have submitted to his leadership, it definitely has revealed God's protection for our family."

When the Cases first married, for example, Susie wanted to stay in the city every weekend and get involved in a church there. But Bob, a competitive barefoot water-skier, wanted to spend every weekend at their lake house in Connecticut. At the time, Susie was angry with him because she thought he was choosing a hobby over knowing God. Looking back, however, she can see how God had his hand on that situation. The pastor of the small country church that they attended was a godly man who had a positive spiritual influence on Bob. "I cried for a whole year because I wanted to be in the city where the action for the Lord was," Susie admits, "but what our family needed was not a big-city church. What it needed was this little family in the country taking us under its wing and modeling for us a healthy, functioning family."

Susie often draws upon the biblical instruction on submission when she counsels women in her BSF class. When women with neglectful husbands come to her for advice, she has learned to encourage them to trust God and stick it out: "I also tell them that I am not going to judge them if they don't, but I do know that if they endure, there is a blessing in obedience. Now that I have been counseling women for a decade, it is interesting to see how many of those marriages have ended up strong. So that's a place where Scripture has really kept us out of trouble."

Leading Volunteers

When Susie was in business school, she seriously considered getting a doctorate in teaching. Then, after her son was born, she taught second-year finance at Columbia Business School for three years. She was in class only one afternoon a week for one semester out of the year, but she looked at the position as an opportunity to keep alive her dream of getting her Ph.D. and becoming a professor.

It was while she was at Columbia that she was asked to start a class for Bible Study Fellowship, an international Bible study program, in New York City. She hesitated at first, but she wanted to learn the Bible well, and she wanted Carl to be involved in the children's program. "I was so determined for him to grow up differently from the way I grew up," she explains. "My idea was that I would just help to start it and then some wonderful, mature believer would teach it and I would have just put the labor into getting it going."

That didn't happen. So Susie continued to build the BSF class while still teaching her business course. Then the day came when she knew she had to make a choice. It was the last day of the semester at Columbia, and as she always did during the final session, Susie was planning to present her testimony to her sixty students. What she hadn't planned on was Carl coming down with a fever of 104.5 degrees. Her baby-sitter got very angry with Susie for leaving him, but Susie could see no way out. "I have to go," she told the sitter. "This is spiritual warfare and I just have to be there."

But as she walked out the door, heartbroken at leaving Carl ill, Susie knew she was at a bigger crossroads. "It would have been fun to be a professor and to try to be dean of the school. If I wasn't going to compete in the business world, competing in the academic world looked fun," she says. "But I remember thinking at that moment, *I can't do this. I am going to devote my time to the volunteer Christian world instead because when my kids are really sick, other volunteers will understand and step in.*"

In the years since, she has learned a great deal about how to incorporate biblical principles into work done in a volunteer setting. For example, learning to expect people to give their best even when they're not getting paid was a paradigm shift for Susie. "My experience has been, you work for money and money is your reward," she says. "I have found that it is a very different experience motivating people if you aren't giving them a bonus. But there is such a freedom in learning to do your best, regardless of the compensation. It releases you from thinking that you need to earn God's love when money is not part of the equation."

Susie seeks to motivate her volunteers to perform with passion by encouraging them to view their work as a way to thank God for his gift of salvation. "Part of it is just continually hammering on that message—that you're already loved, you're already forgiven, you're a daughter of the King, and if you give him your best, it is a nice way to say thank you."

Susie spends a lot of time praying for her workers, particularly when problems arise. Once, for example, one of her leaders was dressing inappropriately. "As followers of Christ, we're called not to tempt others by the way that we dress," she says. "In New York, you have to get pretty extreme for your appearance to be eye-catching, but I felt that she had really crossed the line. I was going to talk to her about it, but I felt a prompting to wait a week. And the next week she came in looking like a nun!

"Part of leadership is learning to always talk to God first before you deal with a subordinate on an issue," Susie concludes. "I could have learned that lesson in the marketplace too, but God happened to use the volunteer world to teach that to me."

After a few years, Susie thought she had learned everything she needed to know about managing volunteers. But the lessons are ongoing. Recently, she has gotten much smarter about whom she "hires." "I used to just pick them and then work hard at training them," she says. "Now I am much pickier and there is a lot less training. I know now what style person works better with me and what kind of issues I can tackle."

In the past, for example, Susie intentionally recruited new mothers. She knew how hard it was to quit work cold turkey and she wanted to give them an outlet for interaction with other women. Over time, however, she realized that working with these women could be a logistical quagmire: "They call because they don't have a sitter," she says. "It's hard working with new mothers because it is a tough transition time in their lives, and what they need to do is focus on getting their families running right. When their kids are in nursery school, that is the time for the moms to step up their volunteering."

Closer to Home

Susie also has opportunities to integrate biblical wisdom into her work as president of the board of her building, which is made up of thirty-five individually owned apartments. She doesn't have any dramatic conversion tales to share, but being on the board has given her a chance to show how a person can think through a problem biblically.

Take the size of the building superintendent's Christmas bonus, for instance. The man's union sets his regular wages, but the owners of the building are free to give him a token bonus or a significant raise. "I talked about our relationship with him as a long-term one and got the board thinking not about what we were doing just this year, but what kind of an ongoing relationship we wanted with this person who lives in our building," Susie says. "I tried to get them to see him not as our subordinate but as a person equipped to do something that is critical to our survival. There is a lot in the Bible about employer-employee relationships. It's in the old-fashioned vocabulary of masters and slaves, but it reveals much about how we are to act toward our employees."

The result? After years of token bonuses, the board decided to give the building superintendent an encouraging raise.

Other board issues have more to do with the practical matters of condensed living. For example, the board members had to decide whether they were going to let people with dogs use the front elevator or the service elevator. "There was a broad spectrum of opinion. Some people felt we shouldn't even have dogs in the building; other people thought their dogs should be in charge of the elevator!" Susie says, laughing. Again, biblical wisdom showed the way: "God gave us dominion over the animals, so animals are not in charge. I didn't use that vocabulary, but I did stress that we shouldn't sacrifice some of the tenants' comfort for the sake of the other tenants' pets."

The board decided to allow dog owners to use the front elevator as long as they kept their pets on leashes (to do otherwise would abuse their neighbors' goodwill). And the people who didn't like dogs were encouraged to wait for the next elevator if someone with a dog got on before them. "It sounds like a small thing, but again, when you're living on top of each other, the little things make a big difference," Susie says.

Just Say No

People often assume that women who don't work for a paycheck have all kinds of free time, but that frequently is not the case. Whether it's because they feel guilty for staying home or for some other reason, these women often feel they have to say yes to every organization or charity that asks them for help. But if a balanced life is a priority, that simply is not an option. The key, according to Susie, is learning how to say no.

She learned this lesson the hard way.

The second year she was home, she decided to take Italian lessons. This was on top of teaching at Columbia, spending a lot of time working with another volunteer organization, and leading a Bible study for Campus Crusade's Executive Ministries group. In addition she had a high-energy toddler who didn't sleep through the night for twenty-two months.

"Every night at eight o'clock I would just pass out," Susie confesses. "My husband would come home and be frustrated with how tired I was. But I said, 'What am I going to quit?' The answer was that I should have quit almost all of it. It wasn't working. If you're so tired that at eight o'clock you lie down and pass out for an hour and a half, something's not right."

At that point, Susie decided she needed to get Carl on a regular schedule and learn how to run a household. After that, she would have time for *one* outside activity.

That system worked for a few years, but Susie got increasingly busier as Carl got older. By the time Sarah arrived, she was overcommitted again. When Sarah was thirteen months old (and still nursing), Susie contracted pneumonia and ended up in bed for six weeks. Bob had asked her to stop nursing because she was so run down, but she resisted (she was still learning the concept of submission!). So he took measures into his own hands. One day when Susie was lying in bed nursing Sarah, her husband picked up the child and said, "Your nursing days are over."

"He took her away and that was it. It was time," Susie admits. "The whole time I was in bed sick I knew I was there because God said, 'You said you wanted to do it my way, but you are doing it my way *and* your way.'"

Since then, Susie has learned to set boundaries. For one thing, she makes a point of not taking on responsibilities that are going to leave her husband and children alone when they need her. At one point, for example, she was on a board that held weekend meetings. "I thought, *Won't this be charming? Bob will have time with the kids, I will have time to do the Lord's work, and everyone will be happy,*" she says. "Well, it was a disaster every single time the meetings came around. I thought, *You know what, this is a season in my life in which I just don't have the luxury of checking out three weekends a year and going to a board meeting. There will be time for that, but right now what I need to do is be there taking care of my family on the weekends. That is our time together as a family.*"

Susie does most of her BSF work—lesson preparation, class time, returning phone calls—while Carl and Sarah are at school, which leaves about six hours a week while they're still in school for such things as hair and doctor appointments and coffee with friends. That doesn't leave much time for favorite hobbies like reading and needlepoint, although Susie absolutely refuses to give up her weekly two-hour tennis session.

Over the years, Susie has learned to pay attention to logistics and to let her schedule dictate what she says yes and no to: "I schedule in downtime. I schedule in family time. I schedule in transition time. I look at logistics and say, 'If I do X, Y, and Z, it is going to be a crunchy day.'"

Susie guards her schedule carefully because she firmly believes that God calls his followers to live peaceful, well-ordered lives. "God is a God of calm and order and peace," she says. "It's not that he can't be with us in a crisis, but in general, that is not the way he asks us to live. If you are living a frenetic life—I don't care if you are doing twenty things for church—you are not making anyone want what you have. It's not our job to *make* people want what we have, but we are called to be light and salt, and that's not the way."

To Work or Not to Work?

When it comes to whether a woman with children should stay home with them, Susie doesn't think there's a one-size-fits-all answer. She does know that she could not have had the family she wanted if she had stayed in her former position. "If I had wanted to be one of the twelve senior people at my investment bank, I should have stayed single," she says. "Even before I was a believer I was aware that it was going to work that way. I knew that I would never give my children to someone else to raise, and that if I was going to raise them myself, I couldn't stay in senior management. It just wasn't going to work."

In that sense, Susie thinks she could have been smarter about picking a job when she finished business school. She could have chosen something that had more flexibility than investment banking, which involves high compensation, high visibility, and 110 percent commitment.

The workplace expects performance, and Susie believes this creates tension for women because in many cases, they innately want marriage and children. "It is very hard for women to be put into a situation where performance and relationship are at odds with each other," she says. Take that time when Susie felt she had to leave Carl, with his dangerously high temperature, at home with a baby-sitter. "I knew for those sixty students paying their tuition bill at Columbia Business School that I needed to teach that class," she says, "but I also felt it was wrong to leave that sick of a child with a sitter."

Susie knows many working mothers who really don't want to be in the marketplace but who work either because they have no other option financially, or because they're still trying to earn love and approval. Cultural expectations—from other followers of Christ or from society at large—also can complicate the situation. The mother of one of Carl's friends, for example, loves the fact that she gets to stay home, but every time Susie sees her, she talks about needing to get a job. "Why?" Susie asks. "She doesn't need it to live or for stimulation. The only thing not working in her lifestyle right now is her suspicion that she somehow let somebody down by not using her education full-time for pay. And that is so sad. The world has definitely pressured women into a trap that a lot of them would rather not be in, but they feel they're disappointing too many people if they get out."

On the flip side, Susie believes that the evangelical community has a bias against women in the workplace. "God doesn't just have a couple of molds for women," she says. "God didn't make a mistake when he made us the way he did. If he equipped a certain woman with the skills and the desire to be in the marketplace, that's a fine place for her to be.

"Part of what I love seeing in women's lives is when the package works. There are some neat Christian women who have put it together in a way that doesn't look like Ozzie and Harriet. All the balls are in the air and it's working. Just like the mom who has five kids and home-schools and pulls it together. What matters is pulling it together in a way that is excellent and that fits who God created you to be."

Now that Sarah is in school, the cries for Susie to go back to work have gotten louder. Some of the pressure comes from her family's extended circle of nonbelieving friends, who don't understand how much work goes into running her BSF class. "People think, *Oh, it's a little class, and it takes an hour's preparation,*" Susie says. "But I think that's part of the cross for me. It wouldn't bring glory to God if I walked around talking about how much sacrifice it is to teach his Word. It's not about me; it's about him. So I have to keep my mouth shut."

Although Susie knows she is doing what God has called her to do at this point in her life, her faith is still tested by offers to return to work—offers that have gotten richer the longer she's been out of work. Some have even been for less than full-time work, which wouldn't have taken any more time than she currently devotes to teaching and volunteering. She finds it particularly hard to say no when she evaluates fund-raising requests from parachurch organizations. "I wonder if I wouldn't be help-ing further the cause of Christ more by helping fund ministries than by teaching the Bible," she admits.

She has, however, learned to deal with the offers one at a time. So far, each has had some kind of "fatal flaw," from the fact that the company was a competitor of her husband's firm to a requirement for inter-national travel, which Susie didn't want to do when her children were younger. "When and if God wants me to change my life and work for pay, I trust that the pieces will fall into place and fit with my family's needs, and that there will be someone obvious to replace me in my teaching post," she says simply.

What's Next?

Susie used to be obsessive about having a ten-year plan. When her son was born, for example, her primary goal was getting her family situated in just the right place so that Carl's chances of going to an Ivy League school would be better. "Now we are lucky to have even a one-year plan," she says. "That has been a big change for me—not being scared. I always felt I needed to have a plan because if I didn't, somebody might hurt me or bad things might happen. But God is in control, and nothing bad is going to happen that he doesn't know about and allow for his own purposes. Tragedy happens, but life really does work for good, so I tell myself, 'Relax about it, already!'"

At the same time, Susie is fairly confident that God will have a job for her to do when her children leave the nest because she's clearly not cut out to stay home by herself. Whatever that role is, she's sure it will relate to the passion she's had since childhood—helping women realize their dreams. Her friends think so too; whenever she asks them what she's going to do with the rest of her life, they tell her she's going to be "Norma Vincent Peale."

"I know part of that comes out of having grown up with a mom who had a complicated life and a lot of broken dreams, and wishing I could fix her," Susie says. "Of course I can't fix her, but I can go out and help other women. My guess is that I'm going to end up doing something that gives women hope in a practical way. Teaching the Word is part of it, but I know that what I want to do involves more than just giving out God's Word; I also want to give out practical life skills."

Susie knows she'll probably never run a major investment bank, but she does suspect she will run something at some point. "It just makes sense. Why would God give me all this experience hiring and firing and training and figuring out how to keep an organization going? My dream in business school was that if I didn't teach, I wanted to be an entrepreneur. I actually realized that dream in part when I started this class, and that may be as far as the dream goes. But in my soul I don't feel that is the end."

For now, though, she has to be patient. "I keep trying to jump the gun and say, 'God, what is this thing I'm going to do in seven or ten years?

Can I put the groundwork in place now so the day my children are out the door, I've already got it going?' And every time I've tried that, I've failed. I've had several experiences in volunteer ministry where I've really flopped—I didn't get anything done; I wasn't effective; I had conflict with other people. Sometimes I think I should take some classes or something, but God is saying, 'Do what I asked you to do today. I have promised to take care of you today, tomorrow, and for all of eternity, and I will never break that promise.'"

7

Allyson Hodgins

MANAGEMENT CONSULTANT/
ORPHANAGE FOUNDER

IT WAS AN UNUSUAL REQUEST TO COME FROM someone in Allyson Hodgins's position.

A 1999 graduate of the J. L. Kellogg Graduate School of Management at Northwestern University—one of the most prestigious business schools in the country—Allyson was into her second year with the Towers Perrin consulting firm in San Francisco. She was a single woman with very few strings tying her down, and her future was in the palm of her hand. But instead of reaching for the brass ring of career advancement, the thirty-four-year-old Canadian chose what some might consider a bewildering alternative.

She decided to ask her boss if she could move back to Canada and continue consulting in the United States on a part-time basis. While this might seem like a reasonable petition for a mother with young children, it's not exactly the path you expect a highly intelligent, upwardly mobile, unmarried management consultant to take. That is, unless that management consultant is Allyson Hodgins.

Allyson wasn't interested in part-time work so she could devote more time to gardening or shopping. Her plan called for her to take sixteen weeks of unpaid leave each year so she could spend concentrated amounts of time working with Children's Aid International Relief and Development (CAIRD), a nonprofit organization based in Edmonton, Alberta, that runs Father's House, a series of small orphanages in Romania.

She bounced the idea off a mentor at work, and after he indicated his approval, the two of them went to talk to her boss about it. Much to Allyson's surprise, the boss's reaction was identical to that of her mentor. "You know how Jesus describes his knocking at the door and patiently waiting to be invited in?" she asks. "I felt very much like that; that it was not so much the asking of my boss that made this all happen, but my hearing God's call to more fully pursue my passion in Romania. I recognize now how perfect the timing was, and how it was God who had patiently waited for me to build the courage to accept his invitation."

Allyson's decision to work part-time was difficult, not because she didn't want to cut her consulting schedule, but because if she had her druthers, she might spend all her time working with CAIRD. Since helping to found the organization in 1996, she has spent countless hours, both from home in North America and in Romania, helping to get CAIRD off the ground by establishing a firm foundation of love and grace in the orphanages, combined with sound operational principles.

At the same time, Allyson also believes God has called her to the business world, and she would no sooner ignore that call than she could withhold a hug from one of the precious children at the orphanage. Her present working arrangement allows her to give both worlds her best. Instead of helping clients figure out how to retain their employees by day and e-mailing Romania with advice and guidance in the evening, she now takes a month or two off between consulting assignments to focus solely on her nonprofit work. "Some people feel called to full-time work in the nonprofit world, and I believe that will define me someday," Allyson says. "For now, I know that consulting provides me the financial basis to help support the orphanages in these early years, as well as the opportunity to learn new skills, to serve our clients, and hopefully, to impact the lives of my colleagues."

Allyson knows she is likely impeding her career progress by doing what she's doing; it will take much longer for her to become a partner in a firm if she works just 70 percent of the year. But contentment isn't hard to come by when she looks at the faces posted on her refrigerator door or sifts through her memories of the children in Romania. She remembers the two sisters who were living in a decrepit shack in the forest with their alcoholic father before they came to Father's House: the picture of them praying over their first bowl of soup in the orphanage is indelibly etched in Allyson's mind. Or the young boy who was rescued from a state orphanage, where the children are so lost in their own pain that they rarely play with or relate to other children. A video of this child, who now lives at Father's House, walking hand in hand with another boy and helping his new friend up when he falls is, for Allyson, proof positive that she is investing her life in what matters most: bringing love and hope to those who so desperately need it.

Allyson's somewhat unconventional approach to her professional life stems from her philosophy of how faith and work fit together. She considers her life's work to be what she does for Christ. And her business career, though important, is just one piece of that work. "I understand the priorities," she explains. "And because I made that decision early on—that my life would be focused on what I could do for Christ and not on how successful I could be—I evaluate the investment of my time, life's most precious commodity, in perhaps different ways from my colleagues at work."

Putting the Pieces Together

Allyson's first job, washing dishes at a banquet hall, began when she was in seventh grade. That same year, during a school trip to Russia, she began to realize that there were millions of people in the world, many of them thousands of miles away from her home in Edmonton, who were much less fortunate than she was. And with that realization came an intense desire to "give back" in some tangible way. Allyson always has had a penchant for setting and achieving goals, and she quickly added this need to make a difference to her list of life objectives.

For a time, however, it took a backseat to a few other goals. She wanted to excel at her beloved sport of figure skating. Excel she did; years of 5 A.M. wake-up calls to be at the rink by six led her to be a part of a thirty-member precision skating team that won several championships, both in Canada and in the United States. She wanted to become a successful businesswoman, so she went to college, earned a degree in business administration, and spent seven years working in sales and marketing with IBM. Next on the list was her lifelong dream of getting an MBA, so she left IBM, went to Kellogg, and earned a master's degree.

Allyson didn't work on achieving these goals simply so she could mark them off a list and move on to the next one, however. She looked at each step as a way to develop her gifts and to hone the leadership, communication, and problem-solving skills that she already possessed. "Because I wanted to give my best to Christ, I wanted to take advantage of opportunities, be it working for an excellent company like IBM or going to a top-ranked business school," she says. "It just so happens that those things are judged by the world's standards as marks of success, but that's not how I've looked at them, nor why I pursued them. I wanted to know, 'Where can I go to get the best skills? Where can I learn from the best people?'"

This desire to polish her skills and learn from accomplished business-people was developed early. Allyson spent a year in Japan between her junior and senior years in college, participating in an international job exchange program. She decided to pursue the program because at that point, becoming a successful businesswoman was the only thing she had on her mind. But that year in Japan had an unexpected and profound impact on her life.

Allyson's assignment in Tokyo was to work on a joint-venture project between NTT (the Japanese telephone company) and Ameritech. The objective of the project was to produce, market, and distribute a tele-phone directory for English-speaking people in Japan. Ameritech's rep-resentative on the project, Carolyn Jennings, was Allyson's boss, but she eventually became her mentor and lifelong friend.

Allyson had grown up in a church-going family, but she spent most Sundays honing her skating technique at the ice rink. She always assumed she would make a personal decision about whether she believed in Christ when she became an adult, so she didn't spend a lot of time thinking about it. But living in Japan, far away from the church-oriented society she had taken for granted, prompted her to think seri-ously about spiritual issues. At the same time, she had a chance to see faith in action through the example of Carolyn, a committed follower of Christ who often drew from biblical principles as she worked through the complicated challenges of doing business in Japan.

For example, as part of the joint-venture project, Ameritech was responsible for producing the content for the telephone books, and the

Japanese company was responsible for distributing them. During the course of the project, Carolyn and Allyson learned that a number of telephone books that supposedly had been distributed were, in fact, sitting in a warehouse. Carolyn knew that open conflict was not part of the Japanese style of doing business, but she also knew that she had to address the problem. After all, advertisers had been given a certain circulation figure when they signed up to be in the book, and that figure would not be met if the books were not distributed.

Rather than storm into a meeting and demand to know why her joint-venture partners were not holding up their end of the deal, Carolyn handled the matter gracefully yet explicitly, ever respectful of the Japanese style of communication while making sure she made her point. "What struck me about Carolyn was her being centered and having a strong moral and ethical point of view, based on a deep-rooted understanding of biblical concepts," Allyson says. "For the first time I saw someone who directly applied the teachings of Christ to her daily professional life. These teachings affected how she handled problems, how she dealt in patience and love, and how she presented ideas in a graceful yet direct and honest way, which was very different from how things were done there."

Allyson, who naively had assumed that life in the business world would be straightforward and honest, was fascinated by Carolyn's approach to doing business. "Her compass was just what I needed, and that compass was Christ," Allyson says. "I realized that I did not want to go through my life—my business life or any other—without having Christ as the foundation. I realized I could not and did not want to do it myself."

When Allyson looks back at meeting Christ in Japan, she's reminded of the story of Lydia's conversion in Acts 16:14. Lydia, an influential textile merchant in the Macedonian city of Philippi, had been a "worshiper of God." But it wasn't until "the Lord opened her heart to respond to Paul's message" that she became a true follower of Christ. "It's that whole idea of opening my heart," Allyson says. "In theory, I had grown up believing, but I never had that personal connection and relationship. It had not been modeled to me before. So even before I started my official business career, that was something I knew I needed to pursue."

A New Mission

A few months after Allyson graduated from college, she went to work for IBM in Edmonton. At the same time, she found a Baptist church and began growing in her newfound faith. She also began to build relationships with some people who would go on to play a very important role in her future. Early on, she met a young nurse named Haley, and a few years later, she came to know a teacher named Peter Mrazik. Peter, who eventually became Haley's husband, had gone to Romania on a missions trip in 1992. While there, he was struck by the plight of the orphans—more than ninety thousand of them—who were trapped in poorly funded, understaffed government orphanages.

When Allyson went on her first missions trip to Romania in 1995, one of her primary goals was to help women with business development ideas. "I'm very practical, so I thought, *What can I offer?*" she says. "I had a desire to help women who were less fortunate, and to give them the kinds of skills they need to help themselves."

While there, however, a series of visits to state-run orphanages broke Allyson's heart. Although physical conditions in these orphanages had improved somewhat since they made international headlines in the early nineties, there still was a desperate shortage of money and staff to adequately care for the children. "I walked into a dormitory full of cribs where children lay in their smelly, soiled clothing, waiting hours and sometimes days to be changed," Allyson says. "Though the staff worked hard, there often was just one person to care for fifteen or twenty babies. But as bad as the dormitories were, it was actually the playroom that haunted me the most. It was like being in the workshop of a toy-soldier maker. The children would sit on the floor, lifeless, hollow, alone in their world of despair. The only way to bring these children to life was to pick them up and hold them. Unfortunately, when I selected and gave affection to one child, the untouched children, pierced by yet more rejection, would aggressively grab on to me, longing for the tenderness they had never received. It was in the midst of this hopelessness that I heard God's cry for me to dedicate not only my business mind, but more importantly, my heart and soul to Romania."

The following year, Allyson teamed with Peter and Haley to form

CAIRD. During its infancy, the organization primarily worked in state orphanages and helped other groups build private orphanages. In late 1999, however, Allyson and the Mraziks used all the knowledge, contacts, and money they had scraped together to open their own orphanage. Located on a quiet residential street in Medias, Romania, the main home is actually a combination of two apartments in a square, two-story triplex. Purchased by CAIRD for thirty-four thousand dollars, this two-bedroom, two-bath residence is now home to six children, while another five are divided between two other homes nearby. The children, all of whom were either rescued from state orphanages or taken from families that were about to abandon them, range in age from two to eighteen. CAIRD has nine full-time employees, including five caregivers, a cook, an accountant, a social worker, and a building administrator, as well as a part-time tutor. In addition, there are usually at least two Canadian volunteers at the homes at any given time.

Although CAIRD is a charitable organization, it is just as much of a start-up as any new dot-com in Silicon Valley. And although its primary business has more to do with diapers than digital technology, it faces many of the same issues. As financial manager, for example, Allyson must figure out how to meet the monetary needs of the home (by raising money from individuals, companies, and foundations) and pace its growth to ensure that the organization can take effective care of the children. Since companies thrive on the strength of their leadership, CAIRD's ultimate goal is to create a new generation of leaders in Romania. These will be young men and women who have triumphed over abandonment because they know that they are deeply loved. "We see the young people who live and work in our homes as being both the future and the hope for Romania," Allyson says. "Our goal is to ensure that we have the love, the grace, the structure, and the people to make this dream a reality."

Allyson helps to achieve this goal in part by drawing from her business school education, her work experience, and by seeking advice from trusted friends. "What I've discovered is that the only credential that matters really is our personal affiliation with Christ, because he is the ultimate counselor," Allyson says. "For example, one of the reasons university-educated CAIRD President Peter Mrazik has chosen to be a baggage attendant for Air Canada is because of the travel benefits. Yet his Christ-centered vision for CAIRD and his ability to communicate and wisely execute that vision are comparable to those of the many Fortune 500 executives I heard speak or studied while at MBA school. In the end, it's all God's work, and I feel privileged to be a small part of fulfilling God's desire to rescue, heal, and love his beloved children in Romania."

Blending Faith and Work

One of the things that Allyson loves about her work with CAIRD is the opportunity to employ people who might not be able to find work anywhere else because of Romania's troubled economy. On the other hand, as a consultant she often finds herself in the midst of situations where the only solution is to *cut* jobs. Allyson doesn't relish the thought of being a "hatchet person," so she has had to figure out a way to deal with that part of her job while staying true to her biblical values and principles.

One such case involved an oil company that had been on a spending spree for about ten years. Staff numbers had gone up, but returns had gone down. And Allyson's job was to help company executives find ways to cut costs. As she evaluated the problem, she realized that it was not just one, but a series of poor choices and investments that had been made over the past decade. For example, the oil company had hired more employees than it needed to sustain the revenues it was generating. As a result, some employees were left with time on their hands to take training that they might not have needed or used.

Allyson and her colleagues were hired not only to identify specific areas where the oil company could cut back, but also to help the company's leaders learn how to make good choices that would prevent future problems. And this is where Allyson's scriptural foundation guided her actions. She decided to emphasize the biblical concepts of wisdom, discernment, and self-control, as well as the ramifications when staff didn't practice such concepts. She explained it like this: "We're putting the company on a diet because it's been overeating for ten years. So when you ask me what the problem is, my answer is, 'I'm sorry, but you can't eat as much.'"

"Yes, there were people who as a result did lose their jobs, but at the same time I think that what we did was ensure that such layoffs wouldn't happen again," Allyson says. "That was a challenge, but I think it's important to look at problem solving from a preventative and long-term perspective."

Blending faith and work involves recognizing God-given gifts and abilities and then finding opportunities to use them. That might be developing a strategic growth plan for Father's House or helping an oil company figure out how to cut costs. But it's not just what Allyson does with her gifts that matters; "It's the *way* you do things that is important," she says. She cites Romans 12:7–8, which says that if a person's gift is giving, she should "give generously"; if his gift is leadership, he should "govern diligently"; and if her gift is showing mercy, she should "do it cheerfully." Allyson responds, "As Christians, we have a concrete way to show how Christ has made a difference in how we conduct our business and personal lives."

The biblical image of the potter and the clay (see Isa. 64:8) also fits into Allyson's philosophy of faith and work. "Certainly in the business world, things are always changing," she says. "It's important for me to recognize that no matter what the situation is, I'm a vessel for Christ. So if at the last minute clients change their needs, then let me be gracefully molded to help them in a different way."

This attitude of flexibility allows Allyson to take things less seriously: she doesn't slack off in her work, but she also doesn't stress out about matters beyond her control. In the consulting field, for example, when one project is done, a consultant starts on another. And the nature of the project often determines a person's level of happiness throughout the duration of the assignment, not to mention the skills she's gaining and the type of exposure she's getting. Allyson has friends who get upset when they're assigned a project that they don't want. But she looks at it differently. "In every project, there are parts that are challenging and exciting and other parts that may seem more routine," she says. "Hopefully there is more excitement than routine, but each project always delivers a blessing, be it an awesome project manager or a new problem-solving approach. God never leaves us wanting for anything. Sometimes we just need to look a little harder for his blessing."

Allyson's positive outlook and joyful attitude have made an impression on her coworkers at Towers Perrin. In fact, a few colleagues have nicknamed her "the Ambassador" because of the way she frames questions and discusses issues. Once, for example, a friend was given an assignment that she didn't want, and she went to Allyson for advice about how to handle it. In her usual manner, Allyson tried to focus on the positive aspects of the project, but she also encouraged her friend to create options. "When you speak to your boss about this," she told her friend, "don't just say, 'I'm not really interested in this project.' Instead say, 'As you know, this is not my first preference. While I am happy to complete this assignment, I think I could be more helpful elsewhere. In fact, I know of another person who has not yet had this kind of opportunity, and I just wondered if you had considered including her in the project.'"

With advice like that, it's no wonder Allyson's friends call her the Ambassador. Although they mean it only as a friendly nickname, she sees a deeper application. It comes from 2 Corinthians 5:20, which says, "We are therefore Christ's ambassadors, as though God were making his appeal through us."

"When I think of an ambassador, I think of someone who is a chosen representative, a diplomat, a person who is knowledgeable about his or her country and is interested in sharing information and establishing relationships," Allyson reflects. "The ambassador sets an example. If I look at myself in this light, it reminds me that I am a chosen representative and that my actions are evaluated and attributed to the country or belief that I represent. Christ is making an appeal through me, and I want to present Christ in the best way that I know how. I recognize that this is not only a cherished privilege but also an awesome responsibility. I do not take this privilege lightly, and I desire to make a positive impression so that others will feel comfortable with me and want to know more about what I represent."

Another way in which Allyson's faith impacts her work has to do with the companies and people for whom she has chosen to work. In her spiritual life, she has chosen to follow Christ and his teachings, and she uses them as the standard when she evaluates job offers. First, she wants to work for companies with solid values. IBM not only provided many growth opportunities for a young woman just out of college, it also was a company known for having such values along with a strong reputation in the community.

Allyson also wants to report to a manager she can trust. "Do I respect this manager in the same way in which I look at Christ and say, 'That's the teacher I want to have'?" she says. "In the business world, we don't always have that luxury—nobody is ever going to be Christ. But when I was at IBM, that was the thing I appreciated most—my boss was a person from whom I could learn. And I joined Towers Perrin because the woman who was the leader in the office where I worked was someone I admired and respected."

Commitment—to Christ, to her employer, to her closest friends—is important to Allyson. But commitment, at least to a particular company, doesn't seem to be as important in the New Economy as it was ten or fifteen years ago. When Allyson joined IBM, for example, people could expect to stay with the company for twenty-five years and be rewarded for their longevity. But in this era of fiercely negotiated stock-option packages, people are more likely to jump from one company to the next for purely selfish reasons.

Allyson doesn't believe in sticking her head in the sand and pretending that this job environment doesn't exist. But she does believe that a person should think through all the ramifications before taking another job, asking herself, "'Am I jumping from this company to this company solely to get rich quickly, or do I really feel called to do that? Is there something unique that I can provide? If I leave, have I built enough of an infrastructure, have I shared enough of the vision, so that things don't collapse behind me?'

"I think about Christ," she says. "He had only a certain amount of time. He moved quickly, and he went from place to place. But he left that legacy behind. He transferred the knowledge to the people who needed it to be able to continue the work. For me, what I'm looking for is a combination of being faithful, honoring commitments that I have made, and at the same time, being ever watchful for opportunities."

A constant attitude of prayer also guides Allyson as she attempts to live out her faith at work. In addition to specific periods of time devoted exclusively to prayer, her focus includes an ongoing conversation with God throughout the day. "I believe that no matter is too small to present in prayer," she says. "While God might be indifferent to the specific recommendation that I make to a client, I find that the act of prayer centers me and better enables me to present the recommendation in a way that is pleasing to God."

Prayer has helped Allyson maintain a godly approach to ambition, a task that became increasingly important as she was getting her MBA. It had been her goal to go to business school, but she put it off for a few years longer than most people do because she was so involved with starting CAIRD. By the time she was ready to start thinking seriously about graduate school, she was working for IBM in Toronto. She applied to the top Canadian school, but she also submitted applications to the top two U.S. schools, thinking that a degree from one of them might eventually open doors to innovative philanthropic organizations and other funding sources in the United States.

Applying to business school forced Allyson to do a personal ambition check and determine why she really wanted to get her MBA from a top school. "I had to ask, 'Is it my ambition to want to go to the best business school, or is it God's plan for me?'" She tried to answer this question honestly in the essays she submitted with her applications. "God deserves the very best, so if I have the opportunity to learn from the very best, to go to the best school, if the door opens, I'll do that," she wrote. "The onus is on me to continue to keep the focus on God."

When Allyson graduated with her bachelor's degree in 1990, Canada was in the midst of a serious economic recession and jobs were scarce. IBM typically hired at least ten new college graduates in Western Canada each year; that year, Allyson was one of only two hired. When she graduated from Kellogg, however, the job opportunities were practically endless, and the money employers were willing to pay was exponentially greater than what she was used to.

Allyson believes God creates each person as an individual, and she's never been one to compare herself to others. But as she was wrapping up her MBA degree, she was tempted to compare herself to her colleagues. Through this process, she had to consciously replace questions such as "What firm is she going to work for?" or "What is his base salary?" with questions such as "Am I making the progress that I think God wants me to make?" and "Am I making the right choices?"

"Business school was a very tempting environment, and it was hard not to compare," Allyson admits. "But since I knew where my grounding was, what my focus was, it was like having the armor of God on me."

It would have been easy for Allyson to accelerate her standard of living as her income level increased. But she has always had a low-cost lifestyle, and she has made it a point to keep it that way. Her former apartment in San Francisco (she has since moved back to Edmonton), though tastefully decorated with Asian and African works of art, was very simple. And although she doesn't limit herself to eating beans and rice every night, she is conscious of her spending habits. For example, if she goes skiing with a group of friends, she doesn't just fork over fifty-four dollars for the lift ticket without a second thought. Ever present in the back of her mind is the thought that that same fifty-four dollars would pay the salary of one of the employees at the orphanage for almost a month: "I believe in having the basics, but beyond that, I'm very mindful of what I spend."

Mustard-Seed Approach

From Allyson's perspective, these are exciting days to be in the workplace, especially for women who are followers of Christ. "Whether it's my generation or where I work, I see a real genuineness in the work environment," she says. "Because it's a time of change in the business world, people are more open to talk about things. Religion is not a taboo topic anymore, and what we are talking about more these days are real-life issues and how those issues relate to faith."

People typically don't just charge into a discussion about faith, however; the subject usually comes up as part of another conversation. For Allyson, that conversation often centers on her work in Romania. "Before we actually had the home and before I had pictures of the children in my cubicle, people knew of the things I was doing but it wasn't necessarily a conversation starter," she says. These days, however, Allyson's coworkers often find it hard to resist asking questions about the dark-haired little boys and girls whose pictures decorate her workspace.

As a result, four of the eleven children at Father's House now are sponsored by Allyson's female coworkers at Towers Perrin in San

Francisco. "One is a partner of the firm who is married to a pastor and is herself a new Christian—this has been an opportunity for us to talk," Allyson relates. "Another is a single woman who is working through issues relating to wanting to be married and growing up in a Christian home but not yet defining Christianity for herself. This is a way for her to think about someone besides herself and to really connect with a child. The third woman shared with me that this is a way for her to be able to step back from constant analytical work and think about what's really important in life. And the fourth is a young married woman who wants to be more involved in volunteering, and seeing me do this work inspires her to move ahead."

But the connection between Father's House in Romania and Allyson's work world runs two ways. She isn't satisfied with simply sharing stories about the children with her coworkers; she also feels compelled to use every ounce of business expertise she has gained from her time in the workplace and at business school to develop CAIRD and improve the operation of the orphanages. In 2000, for example, she and her partners worked on salary requirements and job descriptions for their nine full-time employees, from the childcare workers to the accountant. "This is what I love about being able to take business concepts to Romania," she says. "The idea of having a career is just not something that exists there. When you've spent most of your life living in a communist economy, the concept of pay for performance is very new and different."

So the CAIRD board is introducing its Romanian employees to the idea of setting goals, and their compensation will be based on how well they meet those goals. This process is complicated by the fact that the inflation rate in Romania is extremely high—in 2000, it was expected to be 20 percent but was actually closer to 40 percent. "We're constantly increasing the salaries," Allyson says.

Setting this type of structure in place early is important for the growth of any start-up. It also takes concentrated amounts of time, which is why Allyson decided to reduce her consulting commitments to thirty-six weeks per year.

The work, however rewarding, hasn't always been easy. Some people have questioned what CAIRD is doing in Romania because, despite the fact that there are so many children in need, the organization brought fewer than twenty into its home during its first year of operation. "One of the biggest challenges that we face with the orphanage has been to determine the pace with which we expand our home to invite more children into it," Allyson admits. "This is a challenge that any start-up faces. Investors and other stakeholders are always looking for the impressive numbers, high sales, fast growth, or numbers of children saved. But I think we can get sidetracked by the need to 'prove' ourselves quickly by showing short-term results, or by showing that there is a need and that we are the best company or organization to fulfill that need. As any international businessperson understands, it takes years to really, really understand the culture and the subtleties of working in another country."

Allyson knows that in her head but confesses, "When my heart speaks, I feel the pain of a child lying alone in a crib in the state orphanage, and there's a driving passion for us to grow as quickly as we can. There is nothing more joyous—to me or to God—than rescuing another child from a life of poverty and spiritual barrenness."

There are no easy answers. "As we continue to grow, we ask God to guide us in the delicate balancing of foundation building and growth," Allyson says. "One of the biblical principles that I am always reminded of is that those who are faithful in the small things will be given more. My prayer is to be given more children to love.

"For CAIRD, we believe that 'one child is so much,' meaning that our focus is on saving one child at a time. It is really a mustard-seed approach, one that cares and cries for the soul of an individual. We're small right now in terms of the homes and the children we serve. But success on a small scale is rewarded with the opportunity to use the approach on a larger scale. That is what Jesus teaches us in the parable of the talents, and it is a truth that applies as well to building orphanages as it does to the growth of McDonald's or Starbucks."

8

Goldie Rotenberg
REAL-ESTATE ATTORNEY

UNREMARKABLE.

That's the comment Goldie Rotenberg's doctor used to write in her medical record when she went in for checkups. Given the word's sometimes negative connotations, that notation always struck Goldie as somewhat humorous. But for the doctor, it just meant that he had nothing to note about her health on that particular day—nothing unusual or out of the ordinary.

Although that description might have been appropriate for Goldie's medical record, it in no way depicts the rest of her: her unforgettable personality, her illustrious career, her persistent faith. In fact, it's difficult to spend five minutes with this longtime New York real-estate attorney without realizing that she is one fascinating woman.

Goldie tends to disagree, of course. "In many ways, my life is not very extraordinary," she says. "Even with the struggles, with the success, I'm really just living it one day at a time. Any step by itself is not particularly noteworthy."

Maybe not, but there have been many series of steps along the way that have been nothing short of remarkable. She's taken tough stands at work. At fifty-two, she's achieved heights of success that many female attorneys who graduated from law school in 1975 couldn't have imagined. And she's remained a committed follower of Christ in the face of opposition—both from her family and at work—that would have caused many people to wilt like yesterday's daffodils.

Goldie, you see, is a Hebrew Christian. She grew up in a Jewish family, the child of Holocaust survivors, but she became a believer in Jesus when she was twenty-six. It was a decision she desperately did not want to make; she knew her friends and family would think she was crazy and do everything they could to change her mind. But once confronted with the truths of Scripture, she felt she had no choice.

Afterward, rather than run for cover in the evangelical world, Goldie decided to remain immersed in the Jewish community. Although she now serves as counsel for a real-estate investment company in Manhattan, she spent most of her career at law firms composed primarily of Jewish lawyers, and she has maintained close ties with Jewish friends and colleagues throughout the years.

"I'm very comfortable in the Jewish community—it's my culture," she says. "But it's a tough place to be. As a Hebrew Christian, you live with one foot in each world. You're sort of an outcast in the Jewish community even though you may be—in education, in cultural understanding, in language, in literature—more well versed than some people who are more religious Jews. You're still damaged goods in some way, still sort of an iffy member. But when you get into the church, you're still a little strange there too."

Goldie's active involvement with Chosen People Ministries, a mission devoted to evangelism among Jewish people, has helped maintain her sanity in her bifurcated world. She's been on the organization's board of directors since 1984. And her keen sense of humor—she gets a kick out of being the self-appointed court jester in business meetings and other settings—has helped her survive in a world that often doesn't know quite what to think of her.

"It's probably made a few enemies in my life, but I don't think there's anything that's so sacred that it can't be made fun of, that's not an allowable target," Goldie says. "I can tell you it's probably my best defense mechanism for my own emotional distress: never let anything get beyond the reach of humor. It's a way to deal with the pain."

During the many years that Goldie was practicing at a real-estate law firm, nearly every client came to know she was a believer by the time she closed his or her deal. But she always established herself as a highly competent lawyer first; otherwise, anything she said about her faith would have had no credibility. In fact, if a client had sought her out simply because she was a Christian, she would have turned him down in a heart-beat. She feels strongly that just because a person is a believer, that in no way implies that he or she is a skilled lawyer.

"Having the right to take a stand, to take a position, and not have somebody be able to dismiss you as a crackpot is very important," she says. "And that's one of the things that not being a lawyer, but being a *competent* lawyer, has given me: a platform from which I can't simply be dismissed as a crackpot. Because this person put his $10 million deal in my hands and it was successful, how could he then turn around and say, 'You're crazy; you don't know what you're talking about'? He's just had a completely different experience with me."

Before Christ

To hear Goldie talk now, it's hard to imagine that she was once a "screaming atheist" who wanted nothing to do with Christianity. But it would be difficult to understand her faith and, in turn, how that faith has influenced her work and career, without first knowing a bit of her personal history.

Goldie was born in New York City in April 1949, a few weeks after her Polish-Jewish parents immigrated to the United States from Germany (where they had been liberated after World War II). Her early years were spent in a Jewish "ghetto" in the South Bronx—an environment vastly different from the well-appointed contemporary apartment in Manhattan's Upper West Side that she shares today with her pet, Undercat.

The family spoke Yiddish at home; Goldie didn't learn English well until she went to school. In those days, her career goal, if you could call it that, was to be Perry Mason's secretary. "That was what was popular on television," she explains. "I come from a family that historically values religious education. But my parents have no education to speak of—nobody does in my family until you get to my generation. So I think at five, I didn't even know enough to say I wanted to go to college."

Goldie's educational pursuits began in earnest in seventh grade, when she enrolled at a magnet school (one that attracts students with special interests or aptitudes) in Manhattan. This was in the days before express buses and her daily commute to school took an hour and forty-five minutes each way. But to Goldie, it was worth every minute. The education she received there was wonderful, even better than what she experienced at Harpur College (which is now part of the State University of New York at Binghamton). Because her high-school classes were so thorough, Goldie found that when she went to Harpur, she had already covered much of the content in her college courses.

In college, Goldie started out as a science major but dropped that because she couldn't handle physics. She tried various departments in the social sciences division, but most of them required a class in statistics, which, try as she might, she simply couldn't pass. When the end of her junior year rolled around and she still hadn't declared a major, she knew she had to make a decision. Her transcript made clear that she would have to stay in the social sciences division if she wanted to graduate, so, although she hated the subject with a passion, she chose a specialization in history because it was the quickest way to finish school. (And, fortunately for Goldie, history also was the only department in the social sciences division that didn't have a statistics requirement.)

Goldie's next step required some thought. When she began college in 1967, the economy was robust, and universities were full of corporate recruiters who didn't care if the graduates knew how to do anything. They just wanted people with degrees whom they could put in training programs at nice starting salaries.

By the time Goldie finished school, however, the economy had plummeted. The week she graduated, the cover of one of the major news magazines featured someone in a Ph.D. cap and gown pumping gas. It was the early seventies—the era of wage controls, price controls, and Vietnam War protests—and corporate recruiters no longer filled campuses. To get a reasonable job, a person had to know how to do something.

Goldie had three options: get a master's degree in history, enter a student services program at another university (with the hope of becoming a dean somewhere), or go to law school. She chose law school practically by default. "My temperament is such that I cannot live with uncertainty," she says. "Sometimes this has worked out very well for me, and sometimes it's a disaster. But I'll make a decision just to have the thing settled. I got my acceptance to New York Law School, so that was it. I had someplace to go; it was a reasonable thing to do; I could afford it if I lived at home—end of discussion."

When her family asks, Goldie has another explanation for why she went to law school. Her father ran a sweater mill, and when she was growing up, Goldie used to spend time there on weekends and during the summer. She'd wander around the plant, and because she was the owner's daughter, all the employees wanted to talk to her. Of course, when they were talking to her, they weren't working, which tended to upset her father. "His expression of that to me was, translated from Yiddish, 'If talking were a trade, you'd be dressed in diamonds!'" Goldie says, laughing. "So when the family asks me why I went to law school, that's what I quote to them—that my father encouraged me: I decided to make talking a trade."

A Life-Changing Friendship

Shortly after graduating from college in 1971, Goldie took a road trip with a friend to Lancaster County, Pennsylvania. They ended up at a bed-and-breakfast in Smoketown, Pennsylvania, that was owned by Margaret Reitz. When Margaret noticed that Goldie was wearing a Star of David on a gold chain around her neck, she remarked that if she wasn't a Christian, she'd want to be Jewish. "The Jews are God's chosen people," Margaret said.

Having been exposed to quite a bit of anti-Semitism growing up, Goldie was surprised by this comment. "Being the cynic that I was, I said to her, 'Chosen for what—slaughter?' To me, being Jewish was a wonderful thing, but it had a really awful history. And I was living with the product of that—everybody in my family was a little bit crazy."

Goldie thought a Christian was anyone who wasn't Jewish; in her culture, the word was used interchangeably with *gentile*. Her contact with followers of Christ had been very limited, and she had certainly never met anyone quite like Margaret. The two women were from vastly different worlds—Margaret was a quiet, small-town wife and mother who had lived a very sheltered life, while Goldie was a fast-talking, fast-thinking city kid—but they quickly became close friends.

Over the next four years, their conversations, through letters and personal visits, often centered on the claims of Christianity and whether they were still relevant. "Looking back, I don't know how I maintained the position that I held because the same things that convinced me that there was no God are the things I look at now and say, 'How can you look at these things and say there's no God?'" Goldie confesses. "But to me, the things that were grounded in truth were things you could prove scientifically, and God was out of that realm."

At one point, Margaret suggested that Goldie get a copy of the Scofield Bible: "Scofield was a lawyer," she wrote, "maybe you would appreciate his annotations." Ever quick with a sarcastic comeback, Goldie wrote back, "Every profession has its share of fools; lawyers aren't exempt!"

In keeping with her personality, Goldie often punctuated her responses with glib barbs about Margaret's faith. Although the older woman had never met anyone with a mouth like Goldie's, she wasn't put off by her banter. She remained patient even when Goldie was sitting next to her in church, giving a running commentary on the sermon.

In 1975, just after Goldie finished law school, she went to visit the Reitz family for the weekend. That Sunday night, she and Margaret went to see a traveling evangelist present a slide show about his recent trip to Israel. As he talked, he traced the history recorded in the Bible against history recorded in secular history books, pointing out all the biblical prophecies that had been fulfilled that were actually part of the historical record.

Goldie knew history, and she was unable to dismiss what she was hearing. In an article published in the February 1986 issue of *The Chosen People* magazine, she said:

I had looked at God as man's invention and the Bible as folklore. Yet someone had taken the Bible and compared it with history. Confronted with the facts, I knew that I would finally have to admit that perhaps, even probably, God was real. Given the amount of energy I had spent denying God, this was a crushing blow. Four years of my words and wisecracks suddenly dried up. As Margaret and I sat into the wee hours of the morning, we barely spoke. Instead, I sat silently as much of what I'd heard for the past years about a loving God fell into place, a God who cares, a personal God, the God of Israel who was and is and always will be. He is a God of fact as well as faith; He is a God who is real not only for gentle, soft Margaret Reitz, but also for a fast-thinking, overachieving Jewish lawyer from New York.[1]

Logic had taken Goldie as far as it could. The only thing left for her to do was to take a leap of faith. So she decided to accept Christ. "I had come to a point where it was the only reasonable thing to do," she says. "I don't think I could have maintained an intellectual honesty if I had walked away after I had perceived truth to be there."

This decision was very difficult for Goldie because she knew how her family would react. "Even though my parents weren't very religious, we were very Jewish, in culture and in mind-set," she says. "I didn't see any difficulty in being a Jewish atheist—there are a lot of them running around the world. But to my parents, believing that Jesus was the Messiah was perceived as going over to the enemy. There's a lot of anti-Semitism that's institutionalized by the church, even today, and with their Holocaust experience, my parents saw me as a traitor."

At first, her parents thought Goldie's new faith was just a passing phase, so they decided to wait it out. When it didn't fade with time, her mother stopped talking to her, and everyone else in the family (with the lone exception of Goldie's sister) followed suit. They hoped that the silent treatment would force Goldie to change, but it didn't.

Going Public

While her parents were dealing with their daughter's "defection" to Christianity, Goldie was busy getting her career on track and learning how to incorporate her newfound relationship with Christ into her life and work. It wasn't long before her faith took center stage in her career pursuits.

While she was in law school, she got a job as a law librarian at the New York office of Baker and McKenzie, an international law firm. She remained there after she completed law school because the pay was better than she could have earned elsewhere and because she was getting to practice some real-estate law. Topics such as New York civil practice and local real-estate law hadn't been a crucial part of the curriculum at

Harvard, Yale, and Columbia, the alma maters of many of Baker and McKenzie's lawyers. But they were subjects that Goldie had studied at New York Law School, so her bosses called upon her to work on overflow cases in these areas.

In 1979, Goldie went to work for Goldstick Weinberger et al., a mostly Jewish law firm that primarily handled conversions of rental buildings to cooperative and condominium ownership. Goldie had met David Goldstick when she was doing one of her first real-estate deals while at Baker and McKenzie. Two years later, she ran into him at another closing. David didn't remember Goldie's name, but he did remember her. He also had a pretty good idea of what she had been doing since their first meeting because he was good friends with the owner of the title abstract company that Goldie used frequently in her real-estate deals.

When Goldie walked into his office for the closing, David was eating rice pudding—the same lunch she saw him eat every day for the next ten years. Only one of the other parties involved in the deal had arrived, which gave Goldie and David a chance to talk. The conversation changed the course of her career.

"When are you coming to work for me?" David asked.

In those days, female lawyers weren't very common—only 12 percent of Goldie's graduating class from law school had been women—and frequently a question like that was just a come-on. Goldie had a standard answer for such inquiries: "When you make me an offer I can't refuse."

David put down his spoon. "Would you really consider leaving Baker and McKenzie?" he asked.

"I'll consider anything, but it has to be worthwhile," Goldie answered.

At that point, David asked the broker who was sitting at the other end of the conference table if she would mind leaving the room for a few minutes. He ushered her out, sat back down, and proceeded to tell Goldie exactly what was going on at his firm—from the areas of practice they had recently entered to the financial condition of the business.

"I didn't find this out until later, but he said when he met me the first time, he knew that it was only my second deal," Goldie says today. "It was clear I had no idea what I was doing. But he decided that when he had the money to expand, I was going to be the next person he hired because I was a bulldog. When I asked for changes in the contract that he wouldn't make,

I made him explain why. I got my whole real-estate education in that one deal from him, and he thought that if I was that determined, that once I learned something I'd be worth having. So he made me an offer that was real."

The next day, a Thursday, David called Goldie and pressed her for an answer.

"David, that's not fair," she told him. "You've got to give me a couple of days."

"Okay," he said, "I'll give you until Monday."

Goldie knew all the lawyers at David's firm were Jewish, as were most of the firm's clients. By this time, she had begun to go to a Jews for Jesus Bible study, and she also had done some legal work for the group's New York office. As she thought through David's offer, she realized that before she went to work for him, she had to make sure he was okay with her faith and with her involvement in an organization whose sole purpose was to evangelize Jews.

As it turned out, David already knew about her conversion. A few months earlier, Goldie had been interviewed for an article in *New York* magazine about believers in New York City, and in it, she had been identified with Jews for Jesus. When one of David's partners learned he was thinking about hiring Goldie, he gave him the article to read.

But Goldie didn't know this, so Monday morning, she went to see David at his office. As she rode the elevator, she passed one of the partners saying good-bye to some clients in the lobby—clients who happened to be members of the Chasidic sect of Judaism. She also noted that every single office door had a mezuzah on it—another indication of just how serious the people at the firm might be about their religion.

"David, do you know what my religious leanings are?" she asked as she sat down with him.

"Yeah, Lou gave me the article from *New York* magazine," he said.

"Are you comfortable with that?"

"Yeah, I don't care," he said. "Don't worry, after you get here, we'll straighten you out."

Goldie persisted. "David, I'm glad that you're comfortable, but I'm going to push you a little bit. You can be flip about it, but if I come, I'm coming with the clients I have—the Reformed Episcopal Church in New York and Jews for Jesus."

"I don't care what you do," he said.

"David, your letterhead that says 'Goldstick Weinberger Feldman Alperstein and Taishoff' is going to go out with a letter from me, perhaps to a Jewish agency, that says 'we represent Jews for Jesus.' That's going to be its opening line if I represent them in a controversy. Are you prepared for that?"

"It's not a problem," David replied again.

Finally, Goldie was satisfied. But she still had to make sure David's key partner was also comfortable with her. (He was the man who had been in the lobby saying good-bye to the Chasidim when she arrived.) So she asked him, "What happens when one of your Chasidic clients says to you, 'I don't want to be represented by a woman'?"

"We'll get rid of the client," he said.

That was it. Her two main issues settled, Goldie went to work for Goldstick Weinberger. It was a big leap, for her and for the partners at the firm. Not only was she a follower of Christ, but she also was the first female attorney the firm had ever hired.

The Right to Speak

Throughout the years, Goldie's administrative skills and her ability to bring clarity to difficult issues has helped propel her to the top of her field. Spurred by these talents, which she is acutely aware are God-given, and under the careful mentoring of David Goldstick, she became the firm's first female partner, and by the time she left in 1989, the name of the firm included hers. These achievements, she believes, have given her a degree of credibility that makes it nearly impossible for people to ignore her faith.

"When women are breaking into a new field or trying to get through glass ceilings, the ones who do it first are those who are twice as good as the men they're competing with," she says. "In this field, I have been good enough so that my competence has been the basis for my platform. Influence comes from a lot of different things: it comes from title and position. And it also comes from competence. People don't easily walk away from competence. And that's granted me my right to speak."

When Jewish clients who are favorably impressed with Goldie's work learn that she's a believer, they invariably ask the same question: "How can a smart lawyer like you believe a foolish thing like this?"

"Everybody thinks he is going to talk me out of it," Goldie admits. "That's what's so wonderful. Everybody, whether he really has a faith or not, thinks mine is crazy and wants to challenge it."

As a result, she's had ample opportunities to explain to colleagues and clients exactly why she believes as she does. Reactions are varied. Some people are too stubborn to even address the issue. Some wonder how someone whose parents went through the Holocaust could possibly become a believer. Some skirt around it because of the emotion involved; even though the Holocaust occurred many decades ago, the scars are deep and memories are still fresh. "Everybody wants to remind me of what the Christians did to the Jews," Goldie says. "And I can't fight that because it's historically true."

Her uncle once told her that when the next Holocaust comes, her Christian friends aren't going to protect her any more than his did. "You have to keep saying to people like that, 'You're probably right,' because they probably are," Goldie admits. "But that charge doesn't address the only question that has any relevance, and that is whether or not Jesus is the Messiah. Nothing else matters."

Faith at Work

The longer Goldie has been in the legal business, the easier it has gotten for her to take a stand when confronted with ethical and moral issues. The first time a client she was representing on a personal matter asked her to bill her services to his business, she had to muster the courage to say no. "It seems like a small thing now, but when I was a young lawyer, it was a hard stand to take," Goldie says. "You never knew if you were going to lose the client over it, or for that matter, if he was going to pay if you didn't bill it the way he wanted."

Fortunately, experience breeds security—both in terms of being a woman in what was once a man's field and being a believer in a nonbelieving environment—and security leads to greater confidence. "Then you can take on bigger issues," Goldie says.

At the same time, Goldie also believes that followers of Christ can maintain their credibility and integrity by being careful not to make moral issues out of things that are clearly business issues. Take staff salaries, for example. "My philosophy is that you should give everybody you want to keep a little bit more than the going rate. They should never be out looking at the want ads. The investment that you make in training is too high," she says. "That's enough of a fight because some businesspeople's philosophy is that whether they are running a public corporation or a small firm, they owe their loyalty to the shareholders and the partners; it's their bottom line that they should preserve, not the staff's salary.

"Can that be raised to a moral issue? Sure, but it's not appropriate. It's not the issue it would be if the staff was not receiving a decent wage."

Along the same lines, Goldie has chosen to treat her employees in ways that she would never expect people who didn't share her values to treat them. For example, law firms, especially larger ones, tend to be hierarchical, and support staff members often aren't treated very well. Goldie says, "The staff is treated like part of the furniture. Actually, the furniture gets treated better—it gets polished. But there's a lot of egotistical behavior. I think everybody has that tendency, but a law firm is the place where you can get away with it because it's structured as if that's the expectation."

Employees of the firms that Goldie worked at—both the Goldstick firm and Goldberg Weprin and Ustin, where she worked from 1989 through 1998—often had to work into the early morning hours on the day a deal closed. Usually, the lawyers went home when they got their part done, leaving the support staff to complete the typing and copying needed for the closing in the morning. "I've never left my secretary or anybody else to work into the wee hours, even though my part was finished," Goldie says. "I don't type, but I'll stand at the copy machine and do the copying so we can all go home at the same time."

Her colleagues thought she was crazy for doing this, but although she never tried to make anyone else do it, Goldie did it because she thought it was the right thing to do. There have been times, however, when Goldie felt compelled to make a moral issue out of something that someone else might have thought was a simple business decision.

Once, when the Goldstick firm was looking for ways to broaden its real-estate practice, one of the partners began doing some commercial leasing work. In the process, he discovered that a client he had begun to represent was actually a front for the Moonies. Goldie could have kept her mouth shut, but she didn't: "I wanted the partner to drop the client. It was a very hard thing. He didn't see the conflict even though it was also contrary to what he believed. But my name was in the name of the firm, and I didn't want to be associated with this group.

"I was doing to him exactly the opposite of what David had done with me when I first came to the firm, when I said, 'Can you tolerate my belief system?' But he could, and in this case, I couldn't. And I had never agreed to."

To her partner, it was simply a business issue. But Goldie refused to relent. "It was a long struggle, but he finally just backed out of it because he wasn't a fighter," she says. "I don't know if he ever agreed—it was easier not to fight with me."

When the dominant culture demands conformity, Goldie admits it certainly would be simpler not to worry whether something violates the biblical command to avoid the appearance of evil. This is especially true of business practices that are marginally acceptable but still legal.

The issues can get very esoteric, Goldie says. "When you're negotiating and you take a position, one of the things that you say is, 'This is my final offer. This point is the deal-breaker if we don't come to terms.'

"But what happens if that's not? Can you say that in negotiating when you know it's not your bottom line? Is that an acceptable way to negotiate in business? It's not the truth. Is it okay? People do it every day. It's a normal part of negotiating—you pretend to draw your line somewhere before your bottom."

Goldie tries not to do this, but she's not always successful. "Sometimes I do it without thinking about it, before or after," she said. "Sometimes I think about it before and I still do it because I find that I'm in a box—the pressure of the moment takes over. But I'm very aware of it—I have a very low guilt threshold."

On Success

In the early years of her career, Goldie was driven to succeed, both to overcome the insecurities she had as a person and to prove that she could make it as a woman in her field. "In my profession, a sign of arriving was to become a partner, to get the owners to change the name of the firm to include your name, and to make whatever the income level is in that year," she says. "I did it. And after that, I was able to relax."

Goldie thinks ambition can be good or bad depending on what a person eliminates from her life to achieve a goal. "I think there's a different level for each person," she says. "I certainly had periods of not-so-healthy activity levels. The best way to deal with ambition is to get there—to arrive at where your ambition leads you. Because once you get there, you can give it up sometimes."

The success that Goldie has garnered in the business world has been a tremendous tool for helping ministries and individuals in a way that she otherwise wouldn't have been able to. For example, she's been able to use her financial resources to support people who really need a break. One such person, a Bible school graduate with a young family, got into trouble because he was naive. He worked for a company that operated coin laundry and other vending machines, and his job was to collect the coins from them. "The people who trained him took money from the collections to pay the tolls going back and forth," Goldie says. "Somehow this kid, who didn't have a bad bone in his body, got caught up in what turned out to be a sweep of a company because there was a lot of stealing going on. The toll thing was a minor problem, but he was an easy target, and he was charged with theft. He didn't know what hit him."

Using her contacts, Goldie found a competent white-collar-criminal lawyer to take the case, and she also gave the young man, who didn't have two nickels to rub together, money toward his legal fees. The lawyer was able to keep him out of jail, and he also fought long and hard to get his record erased.

Today, the young man is a leader in his church and a productive member of society. "If I were doing something else, I certainly wouldn't have had the means to solve that problem," Goldie says. "In that sense, my profession is a platform for doing other things."

Goldie jokingly says that she initially entered the marketplace because "the frog never turned into a prince." With a smile she states: "I couldn't find somebody who could support me in the manner I intended to become accustomed to."

But Goldie believes that remaining single has worked out to her benefit. "There are a lot of things I've done that I could not have done if I were married," she says. "I certainly would not have maintained a marriage well with the time I invested in being a lawyer. I don't think I could have accomplished the ministry things I have done while holding a job and caring for a husband and children. Singleness has given me a lot of freedom to come and go as the opportunities present themselves, and that's been very important to me—and very satisfying."

As she contemplates the role her faith has played in her career, Goldie thoughtfully admits that her life would have been much easier if she had not been a follower of Christ. "I think that's one of the things that believers are afraid to say," she notes. "But my whole life experience has been very uphill in terms of faith. And I don't find that it got any easier in the marketplace than it did in the family. The best you get is tolerance. You don't get acceptance."

As a result, though Goldie continues to believe that Jesus is the Messiah, she has difficulty answering when asked if she's firmly convinced that she made the right choice when she decided to accept Christ so many years ago. "I go through periods of being a bearer of very little faith," she says. "I think we all have our ups and downs, and I think some of my downs are very low. The only thing I can tell you with certainty is that I have so much of my life in the last twenty-five years invested in this point of view, in this community, in this way of living, that I am no longer able to make a really objective analysis. I think that's the bottom line. It would be extremely hard to turn the tables again. Have I ever wanted to walk away? Sure, more than once. Is it really an option? No, I don't think so."

Goldie doesn't waste much time pondering such things. She refers to a line from a favorite book of hers, *Turbulent Souls: A Catholic Son's Return to His Jewish Family* (Avon Books, 1998). The author Stephen J. Dubner was raised by parents who had converted to Catholicism from Judaism before he was born. When he found out he had Jewish roots, he rejected his Catholic background and converted back to Judaism. He got a lot of flak from people about his decision, so much that he began to question whether it was really sincere. Goldie chose a different spiritual path, but she certainly can relate to Stephen's journey. As he describes his story in the book, he writes a line that expresses Goldie's sentiments exactly: "I had given myself many a headache thinking such thoughts, but I realized after a time, you have to tell yourself to shut up and get on with the business of living!"[2]

That, in a nutshell, is what Goldie has done. When lingering doubts or hypothetical questions come up, she just tells herself to get on with the business of living. True, it requires a leap of faith. But ever since that evening long ago in Lancaster County, Pennsylvania, faith has become a crucial part of this ever-logical lawyer's way of thinking. "As you have more experience with God showing up when you think nobody's there, it becomes the thing that you fall back on when your faith begins to sag again," Goldie says, this time with confidence. "It becomes part of your history."

9

Jeanette Towne

ENTREPRENEUR

WHEN JEANETTE TOWNE WALKED AWAY from her position as a second-level AT&T account executive in 1994, she had no idea that she was setting the stage for her future as an entrepreneur.

Quitting didn't make sense professionally. She had been very successful in her sales career since joining the communications giant in 1988. And it certainly didn't make sense financially; the plastics company that her husband owned had fallen on hard times, and her job was the family's only source of income.

At that particular stage in her life, however, Jeanette believed quitting was her only viable option.

The one-time nursing student had worked out of AT&T's office in Modesto, California, until 1992, when, after giving birth to twins, she set up a virtual office at her home. She began telecommuting so she wouldn't have to leave her babies—they had been conceived after an arduous battle with infertility and had spent the first two months of their lives in the hospital after being born nine weeks early.

Even though she worked from home, Jeanette's job required frequent business trips: two weeks in Denver for technical training, three weeks in Cincinnati for sales training, three days in Fresno for corporate branch meetings, and so on. She hired a live-in nanny to help with cooking, cleaning, and other domestic duties, but as the days went by, she found separation from her children and husband increasingly difficult.

By the time the twins, Samuel and Jessica, were eighteen months old, Jeanette couldn't take it anymore. She sought counsel from friends at church who prayed for her during her business trips. One told her, "You know, Jeanette, God is telling me that you have to trust him and quit."

At first, Jeanette thought the idea was ludicrous. She was making $65,000 a year working fewer than forty hours a week. How could she possibly let that go? But the woman was adamant. "You've been asking us to pray, and God is telling me to tell you to quit your job," she said.

Jeanette looked into working for AT&T on an even more limited, part-time basis, but no such job description was available. So, amid the protests of her managers and coworkers, she turned in her resignation. "I had several people tell me, 'You're foolish. You're never going to get anywhere. Why did you do that?'" she says. "And at the time, making that kind of money and not having any other source of income, I admit it does sound a little crazy. But we've got a big God."

The next several weeks were very stressful for Jeanette and her husband, Sam. Most of their savings had gone into his foundering company and their infertility treatments, so they were struggling to get by on very little money. But relief was in sight.

About a month after Jeanette left AT&T, the vice president of her region called to ask if she would be interested in doing some projects for him on a contract basis. The work would take about ten to fifteen hours a week, and best of all, she could do it from home.

So Jeanette secured a business license and became a part-time contractor for AT&T. For the next several months, she spent a few hours each week doing work for her former employer. She spent the rest of her time catching up on domestic pursuits such as sewing and making her own applesauce—activities that she had neglected when she was pursuing a full-time career. "It was perfect," she says of the new arrangement. "I was at home and not traveling at all. I was Mommy of the Week, Mommy of the Month, and Mommy of the Year!"

The project work Jeanette was doing for AT&T eventually turned into account management work, similar to what she had been doing before she quit, only not as time consuming because she shared the job with someone else: "I was making three or four thousand dollars a month working out of my house maybe fifteen hours a week, and spending the rest of the time with my children."

Several weeks after she moved back into the account management role, the person with whom Jeanette was job sharing left AT&T. Rather than hire a replacement, AT&T officials asked Jeanette to do it. "So I hired my first employee at the end of 1995," she says. "I showed her how to do what I was doing, and after she was trained, I stayed at home doing administrative work while she went out and handled most of the customer appointments."

That was six years ago. Today, Jeanette's company, Towne Communications, has more than fifty employees and annual sales of $7 million (compared to $85,000 her first year in business). The firm's headquarters are in Jeanette's new home in Walnut Grove, California, and its corporate administration offices are in Turlock, California. It sells communication hardware and software (voice-mail systems, computer networks, telephone equipment, local and long-distance service, e-commerce applications, and so on) as an exclusive business partner of Lucent Technologies/ Avaya Communication (formerly AT&T) and as a representative of Pacific Bell, MCI, and XO Communications.

Through the exclusive biannual contract that Jeanette signed with AT&T back in 1995, Towne Communications now owns Lucent sales territories from the San Francisco Bay area to the Mexico/California border. "We have retained our original territories and have added more by doing an excellent job servicing our customers, and by achieving phenomenal success in our sales numbers," Jeanette says.

For Jeanette, forty-three, one of the most rewarding aspects of owning her own business is the opportunity to help other women who want to have careers without sacrificing their family lives. Many of her employees are mothers who work part-time from their homes. "There are so many educated professional women out there who were in situations like mine," she says. "They were crying because they had to go to work and leave their babies, but they needed a job."

One by one, largely through word-of-mouth advertising, these women came to Towne Communications, and Jeanette figured out a way to accommodate their needs. Flexible hours, part-time work, job sharing—whatever it takes, she's willing to do it because she believes structuring the company that way is edifying to God. "He has brought us women for whom this is an answer to prayer," she says. "We have an avenue for helping women to work yet fulfill their ministry with their husbands and their children."

Jeanette's family has grown along with her company. In 1997, she and Sam opened their home to two foster children—sisters Sarah, now six, and Amanda, now four—whom they have since adopted. And although the company's work load has increased, Jeanette has been able to maintain her part-time schedule by hiring competent employees and delegating responsibilities to them.

Although she has received enticing offers to sell her company or to go to work for another firm in a senior-level position, Jeanette is content to work out of her home office with her husband, who is Towne Communications' vice president of operations, and several other local employees. At this point in her life, she's not about to exchange the pitter-patter of little preschool feet on the hardwood floor in the living room or the excited chatter of her nine-year-old twins when they come home from school for any amount of corporate status in the world. "I wake up every day and just feel incredibly blessed, *incredibly blessed*," she says.

Overcoming the Odds

With four beautiful children, a loving, godly husband, a roomy new home, *and* a successful business, it's easy to see why Jeanette is so content. But the true depth of her present gratefulness can be mined only when she explains a difficult aspect of her past.

Jeanette was born in Los Angeles, the daughter of first-generation Italian-Americans. Her parents were devout Catholics who placed a great deal of importance on old-world customs and strong moral values. She went to college with the goal of becoming a nurse, but at nineteen, she put those plans on hold when she met the man who became her first husband. Her parents were living in Europe at the time, and without their discerning input to guide her, she naively believed all the lies this twenty-eight-year-old man told her. "I bought a picture that someone showed me, but that's what it was—a picture," she says.

In the years that followed, Jeanette came to learn that she had married a physically and verbally abusive, unfaithful man who also was addicted to drugs and alcohol. "All of the horrible things that could happen to a woman in a relationship—I lived them every day. I experienced all of the stages of domestic violence," she says. "But I had been really sheltered. I had no clue. My parents were great with each other. I figured if I was a better person, or if I cleaned the house better, I wouldn't be hurt. I just didn't think that anyone in the world who was supposed to love me would ever lie to me or want to hurt me."

As Jeanette's personal life deteriorated, she focused more and more of her energy on her career. "The worse that relationship became, the harder I tried to excel at outside things to prove that I was okay, that I really was not a doormat," she says. "That's the one good thing that I took from it."

Jeanette's foray into the field of electronics began with a volunteer position at her church in which she taught junior high students—and herself—how to use Apple computers. That eventually led to a sales job with Motorola. She had very little experience when she went to work for the semiconductor company, but she was eager to learn, and that's exactly what she did. From 1982 to 1985, she took just about every training class Motorola offered, studying everything from printed circuit boards to microchips. "Since I had a science background, I took to the electronics," Jeanette says. "I understood it easily, and I was very excited by it. I thought, *Wow, this is great! They are teaching me something that I can understand and I like, and they pay me to do it.*"

A few years later, the semiconductor industry went south, and Jeanette was laid off from her job with Motorola. She then went to work for Rose Electronics, a smaller firm in San Jose that sold switches, networks, resistors, transistors, and other computer components. She knew nothing about passive electromechanical components before she got the job, but once again, between reading books from the library and taking company training courses, she learned as she went. "I got a break," Jeanette says. "My supervisors knew I had worked for Motorola and my sales results were good, so they trained me and trusted that I would do a good job for them."

While Jeanette was at Rose Electronics, her already abusive husband grew increasingly violent. "He came after me one time with a hammer," she says. "During the attack, I looked up and saw myself in the bathroom mirror, cowering below this person. I began to laugh, and I told him, 'Go ahead, kill me now, because death is far better than life with you.' He promptly dropped the hammer and walked away.

"During this whole time I was going to my Catholic church, and I was always praying, 'God, would you *please* help me?' And then at twenty-nine, I decided that I was better off facing my parents with the truth and the possibility of the dreaded word *divorce* than living that way any longer."

Soon thereafter, Jeanette, with the full support of her parents, who had returned from Europe by this time, obtained a divorce and began the process of rebuilding her life. Her father encouraged her to buy a house so she would have some stability in her life. She couldn't afford one in Silicon Valley; even in those days, real-estate prices were high compared to those in other areas. But with her parents' help, Jeanette did find a small home in Modesto, which is about ninety miles southeast of San Francisco. That's when she started working for AT&T. "God really had his hand on me through all this. It was such a blessing to have a job that was six miles from my home," she says.

At that time, AT&T was hiring people with bachelor's degrees or MBAs. Jeanette had neither—she was still working toward an associate's degree, which she eventually completed by taking night classes while holding down a full-time day job. She did, however, have a proven sales record. "My sales results from the other two jobs were strong. I was completing 200 to 300 percent of my objective," she says. "AT&T wanted somebody who was able to sell technical applications, who had exceptional sales results, and who could pass the SAT-like entrance exam. That is how I got in."

A year later, in 1989, Jeanette met Sam at a business seminar. The two became friends and eventually started dating. Jeanette wasn't a born-again believer at the time, but she began devouring the Scriptures after Sam took her to church for their first date. "I thought, *This is what I have been looking for all of my life. Why didn't someone tell me about this before?*"

After all she'd been through, Jeanette initially had no intention of getting involved with another man. But as she grew stronger in her new-found faith, her relationship with Sam turned serious as well. Today she says, "He's such a solid Christian. He has been such a rock and such a mentor for me."

The couple married in 1990. In addition to going through premarital counseling with Sam, Jeanette also sought faith-based therapy to help her deal with painful issues from her earlier destructive relationship. In the years since, she has gotten more comfortable with talking about her past with other women facing similar situations, as well as with friends and work associates. She sometimes has to swallow her pride, but she realizes that her story is a powerful witnessing tool: "My life is a testimony to Christ and what he has brought me through, and I wouldn't be who I am today if it weren't for that bad experience."

A Christ-Centered Company

That said, it's not surprising that Jeanette has chosen to be candid about the fact that she bases the entire operation of her company on biblical principles and Christ-centered values. When dealing with clients or Lucent representatives for the first time, she jokingly tells them that there are many bosses in the world, but she answers to the "big one," meaning God. "That is my way of stating it without being offensive or sounding like a religious fanatic," she says.

She regularly leads in prayer at corporate meetings between Lucent and Towne Communications. This comes as no surprise to her employees. If they didn't know about her beliefs before she hired them, they do as soon as they read her president's letter on the second page of their employee manual. But praying at mixed meetings can be somewhat risky given that the Lucent representatives hold the keys to the sales contracts that Jeanette's company relies on for its business. "Not long ago, we had a Lucent area manager and our entire southern California team meet at a restaurant for a luncheon meeting," Jeanette says. "As we began to have the food served, I asked if it would be all right if I offered a blessing. The Lucent manager agreed that it would be okay, so I prayed. My employees weren't surprised, but mixing Christianity in today's corporate world can be tricky. This manager awards our biannual contract, and I wouldn't want to risk not getting a contract in 2002 because I offended her in some way. So it's a delicate balance."

On another occasion, in a phone conversation a senior-level Lucent manager at the company's corporate headquarters in New Jersey mentioned to Jeanette that her husband had been critically injured in an accident. Jeanette didn't know anything about the woman's religious background, but she felt compelled to ask if she could pray for the situation. The woman agreed, and Jeanette prayed with her. Later, the manager left a voice-mail message thanking Jeanette for her prayers. "But again, that was very risky because if the manager was closed to the prayer, it might have affected how she thought I would represent Lucent, and it could have had an extremely catastrophic financial effect on my company," Jeanette says.

Speaking of finances, Jeanette has been committed to practicing biblical stewardship in her business since "day one." This includes following Proverbs 22:7—"The rich rule over the poor, and the borrower is servant to the lender"—to the letter. Through the years, Jeanette has been tempted to borrow money to help her business grow. She knows it could have grown much faster if she had secured a Small Business Administration loan, for example. Such loans may be fine for some people, but Jeanette prefers to go without rather than be encumbered by debt. She did without a copy machine for five years because she didn't want to get a loan to buy one. Going to Kinko's to copy documents all the time wasn't very convenient, but it kept Jeanette from becoming a slave to payments.

Jeanette was particularly grateful for this a few years ago when she found out that Towne Communications had a $50,000 tax bill that was due in three weeks. After she paid the bill, the company had a total of four dollars in the bank—a situation that would have been financially devastating if she had been making payments on a copy machine or an SBA loan.

Jeanette also believes firmly in tithing, both personally and on the profits of her business. "We start with 10 percent. We give what we feel God is leading us to give," she says. "That's where my husband has been very strong. He always says, 'You can't outgive God.' I know God has blessed us because we have been faithful. We aren't giving so that he will be faithful, but I believe tithing keeps us unbound financially."

When it comes to partnerships, Jeanette takes the biblical admonition not to be "yoked together with unbelievers" (2 Cor. 6:14) seriously, even if it means forgoing opportunities that would be financially lucrative. After she had been in business for a few years, for example, one of her largest competitors wanted to buy Towne Communications for several million dollars and hire Jeanette to run the area of the country that she covers now.

But the man was not a believer, and Jeanette believed that selling to him would have created an unequal partnership. Not only would she not have been in charge of the business aspects of her company anymore, but she also would have had to give up her moral and ethical control. "There is no way that I would have ever done that, only because I would have been subject to his decisions," she says. "He was an awesome business-person, but on the other hand, he had a reputation for being as sharp as he needed to be to get what he wanted."

Jeanette, on the other hand, believes that it is her duty as a follower of Christ to behave in a way that reflects his presence in her life. That means total honesty in all her business dealings—no fudges or fibs allowed. It also means remaining peaceful during crisis situations, to the point that the people she's dealing with sometimes can't tell whether she's angry because she's not "cussing up a storm" when something goes wrong. When customers call and pepper her with colorful speech because their data switches are down, she calmly listens and tries to solve their problem. "Because I can see the bigger picture, their angry comments are just tiny bullets," she says. "That's all they really are. So I don't tend to get excited about things that really don't matter."

Integrity at Work

It's not always easy to be Christlike at work, however. For Jeanette, one of the most difficult aspects of being a Christian woman in the market-place is dealing with people's tendency to think that because she's a believer, she's weak. Colleagues or competitors may think, *We can get one up on Jeanette—she's not going to speak her mind because she is a Christian.*

That is not true, of course, but Jeanette knows she may have lost her competitive edge at times because she was unwilling to give gifts or trips to key business contacts in an effort to obtain more contracts. "We get a lot of opportunities, but I feel there have been times when we were passed over for additional business territories because someone else was more aggressive," she says.

Situations like this test Jeanette's faith, but the most significant test came early in her career, when she was still employed by AT&T as an account executive. (Although she did not yet understand what it meant to have a personal relationship with Jesus at that point, her strong moral sense of right and wrong was fully operational.) She faced enormous debt after her divorce, and so she decided to take on another job. By day, she was a professional representative of AT&T, meeting with presidents of companies and boards of directors. By night, she was a waitress at a comedy club in a hotel.

About that time, a colleague who worked for a competitor asked her if she would be willing to sell him her embedded base list, a detailed summary of every AT&T customer in central California who was paying rent on the company's equipment. These lists were strictly proprietary—leaking them to AT&T's competition would be grounds for immediate dismissal.

Jeanette's colleague opened up conversations by telling her how much money her list would be worth to him and frequently joked about how she could probably use the money. After several weeks of teasing her about her list, he finally pitched her a price of $8,000. That may not sound like much in today's economy, but given the financial situation Jeanette was in at the time, it seemed like a million dollars. "No one would have known—he would have given me a check personally, and I would have made a copy of the coveted list," Jeanette remembers. "But I couldn't do it! I knew it was wrong and went against every principle that I was trying to live by—that God owned the cattle on a thousand hills, and that he was in control of everything: all of my life, all of my finances, everything."

She eventually turned the guy down. It wasn't easy, but looking back, she knows she did the right thing. "I continued to work the two jobs until I got my feet back on the ground again, and eventually my finances turned around," Jeanette says. "Today I believe that some of God's blessings in my life are there because I have tried to be a good steward of what the Lord has given to me."

These days, Jeanette has much more control over ethical issues because she controls her business. When she was with a previous employer, however, she occasionally had to stick with her principles, even if it meant losing out on sales commissions or bonuses. For example, depending on the type of lease contract a customer had, he could either buy the equipment when the lease period ended or lease new equipment. What many customers didn't know—because the sales reps were encouraged not to tell them—was that sometimes the contracts allowed them to buy the equipment for just one dollar when their lease was up. "Managers said, 'Tell them that they have to buy it out, but don't tell them that the buyout is a dollar,'" Jeanette remembers.

Once, near the end of a year when California's economy wasn't doing so well, Jeanette had a customer who was getting ready to finalize a $200,000 deal with her company. "I found out the day before the end of the year that the customer had one of those dollar leases," she says. "He had already signed papers for the new system, thinking that he had to buy the old one out. That meant about $10,000 in commission plus a bonus for me. But I called the guy up and told him what I found out— and it was killing me; it was absolutely killing me!"

The customer kept the old equipment. But again, Jeanette knew she had done the right thing: "He had told me to come on over and he would sign the paperwork, but once I realized what his contract said, I couldn't do that."

Boundaries

One of the biggest challenges that Jeanette faces as a home-based-business owner is making sure her work doesn't interfere with what she considers to be her most important job: taking care of her husband and four young children. She has set up boundaries to help her accomplish that. For example, she is quite involved with her children's classrooms at school. She takes time off for most field trips as well as for each of her children's birthdays. When people call her on those days, they get the following message: "Hi, you have reached the voice mail for Jeanette Towne. I am not here right now because I am with twenty third graders on a field trip."

This policy also applies to Jeanette's employees, many of whom are believers. "They know that in their relationship with me as a business-person, Christ is first, and that their relationship with their family is second," she says. "When an employee tells me, 'I'm not going to work today because I'm doing this project with my daughter's school,' she knows she doesn't have to say any more. Oftentimes I'll call an employee's voice mail and find that she's on a field trip. I don't ask my workers to report to me at all unless they're going on vacation or they're unable to answer customer calls and they need someone to cover."

Jeanette and Sam arrange their working hours to accommodate their children's schedules. This has taken various forms over the years. At times, they have employed a nanny; other times, they have provided childcare themselves, taking turns watching the little ones who weren't at school or preschool. But even when they have a nanny, as they do now, Jeanette still takes frequent breaks from her work to spend time with four-year-old Amanda. "For me as a working mom, creativity and flexibility are the norm," she says.

No matter how much business Jeanette could attend to, weekends and evenings are work-free time zones at the Towne home: "We have a Monday-through-Friday job. I turn the business phone off on the weekend." It's tempting to fudge on this boundary, but Jeanette refuses to do so. "I don't want to be fifty and say that I spent that extra Saturday in the office when I should have been playing with my kids. I had two children, and I brought two more in: I have to remember that I did that for a reason."

That said, Jeanette has had her share of people who question whether she should be working at all. "My mother never worked outside the home, and when I got pregnant with the twins, the first thing out of her mouth was, 'You're quitting work, right?'" Jeanette says. "How do you tell your mother that your husband really isn't making a paycheck right now? At the beginning, not working wasn't an option."

Jeanette got the same response at church; many of her friends wondered if she was planning to quit her job when the babies came or continue working. She often felt left out when she went to functions for the mothers in the church because she was a career woman and could spare only forty minutes during her lunch hour to attend. But she also had friends at church who were in the same situation she was—many of those women have worked for Towne Communications for several years. Jeanette's first employee, Kathy Salvatore, has been particularly encouraging and faithful. Kathy, a mentor and sales trainer who recently became a partner in the company, had an infant when she joined Jeanette in the business. The two shared the same job, and they provided day care for each other's children when one had outside appointments.

On top of all her work and family obligations, Jeanette still has managed to find time to take some of the courses she needs to complete her bachelor's degree. With such a busy life and so many little people to care for, Jeanette has had to find creative ways to carve out one-on-one time with God. In the early days, "I remember feeling stretched in trying to keep my Bible reading up, especially when the twins were infants," Jeanette admits. "I would fall into bed exhausted and doze off when I tried to read the Word."

Jeanette found that her car stereo held the key to this dilemma. "I bought a great dramatized version of the Bible on tape, and I keep it in my car at all times," she says. "This has been wonderful because I can go through specific books—Old or New Testament—when I feel that is where my study should be. I know that popping in my tape for five or ten minutes as I'm waiting for the kids to get out of class or when I'm en route to a meeting doesn't seem like much, but I am amazed at how much I do read (or hear). This way I know that I am constantly in the Word."

Staying focused on Scripture helps Jeanette maintain her perspective when she contemplates where she'd be if she had stayed at AT&T, or what her life would have been like if she had accepted offers from people who wanted to buy Towne Communications. Had she gone to work for someone who bought her company, she could have been a regional vice president making $250,000 a year. But she also would have been right back where she was before: spending most of her time on the road, away from her family. "I think of it once in a while, sure I do—$250,000 a year is a lot of money," she says. "But I have five people here who are so much more important than $100, $1,000, or even $250,000 dollars!"

Jeanette has a glass door in her office through which she can see her children's bedrooms down the hallway. When she looks up from her work to see Amanda with her nose pressed up against the windowpane, she knows she's right where she's supposed to be. "Frequently throughout the day, I'm able to take hug breaks with my kids, have a snack or lunch with them, or go into my kindergartner's class and hand out cupcakes," she says. "If I was doing the corporate thing for the money, I would have missed that nose against the glass four times a day. You could never have that in the corporate world."

10

Pin Pin Chau

BANK CEO

PIN PIN CHAU NEVER EXPECTED TO MAKE a career out of banking.

A native of Hong Kong, she had come to the United States in 1961 to go to college. By the time 1970 rolled around, she had bachelor's degrees in history and fine arts from a small private college in Iowa, a master's degree in Asian history from Yale University, and an almost-completed Ph.D. in literature, also from Yale. What she didn't have—and what she couldn't seem to find—was a job to tide her over until she finished her doctoral thesis.

She had hoped to secure a teaching position at a university in New York City, where she lived with her husband, Raymond. When that didn't work out, she decided she needed to find a job in the business world, perhaps with a bank or an insurance company because they were the large employers in New York. It was a daunting task for someone who couldn't even type.

While she searched for employment, Pin Pin continued her regular practice of helping out at her small church in Chinatown. The pastor didn't feel comfortable preaching in English, but many of the people in the congregation were second-generation Americans whose limited understanding of the Chinese language made it difficult for them to understand his sermons. So Pin Pin served as his translator.

One Sunday, an executive from a local bank visited the church. As he watched Pin Pin translate, he was impressed with her ability to think on her feet. *If I could get this person to work for me, it would be very good,* he said to himself. When he expressed his thoughts aloud, a member of the church quickly informed him that Pin Pin was, in fact, looking for a job.

She had to look no farther. She went to work for the bank as a platform assistant (or customer service representative).

The transition from a campus environment to retail banking was a difficult one for Pin Pin. Besides not knowing how to type, she had forgotten how to calculate compound interest—and this was in the days before electronic calculators. "My colleagues thought, *This is supposed to be some bright young person from Yale, and she can't even calculate compound interest? She wants to be a banker?*" Pin Pin remembers.

At that time, of course, Pin Pin had no intention of becoming a banker. In fact, the very idea amused her. Growing up in Hong Kong, she had always been a somewhat scatterbrained child who didn't do well with money. If her six siblings ever found cash lying around, they usually gave it to her because they automatically assumed that she had lost it.

Beyond that, the idea of going into business of any kind was foreign to Pin Pin. Though a bit absent-minded, she was highly intelligent and performed well in school. "In those days in Hong Kong, if you were a good student, you studied physics, and if you were a bad student, you studied marketing or business," she says. "So I had never had many thoughts about business."

Working at the bank quickly dispelled Pin Pin's preconceived notions: "I found out that some of the brightest people are businesspeople. Their minds can get into gear very quickly; they are sharp."

Pin Pin also was intrigued by the various constraints and obstacles that different businesses face and how businesspeople can circumvent and overcome these difficulties. She had always been interested in painting and drawing (as a young girl, she had dreamed of one day becoming a cartoonist), and the creativity needed to overcome such challenges appealed to her artistic side. "I think if I had been born in America, I probably would have become a mechanical engineer because I am always curious about how things work," she says today.

Because of her lack of business experience, however, Pin Pin's first months at the bank were trying. "Pin Pin, I've never seen you more miserable than you are now," her husband told her. "Do you want to quit?"

Pin Pin had prayed earnestly for a job, and she knew God had met her need. "Look," she told her husband, "unless he gives me a very clear indication that I should quit, I don't want to."

So she stayed. Once Pin Pin learned everything there was to know about being a platform assistant, she moved into lending, then into branch management, then into international banking and trade finance. And somewhere along the way, that temporary job became a full-fledged career.

Thirty years after she took her first deposit in New York, Pin Pin now is president and CEO of Summit National Bank in Atlanta. This full-service bank specializes in international trade finance, as well as in serving small businesses and a wide range of ethnic customer groups. Given the lack of financial acumen that Pin Pin demonstrated as a child, it boggles her mind that she is now running a bank with total assets of $320 million. She never set out to become CEO of a bank, and although she is one now, she knows she didn't get there on her own strength. "Even when we think something is humanly impossible, when God decides that it should be—then it will be," she says with conviction. "He wants to keep me humble, knowing that everything comes from him. I learned early on that the important thing is to know what God's will is in my life and not to limit God. If he thinks that I'm good enough to be a CEO, I'll be a CEO."

A Personal God

Pin Pin is acutely aware that God has guided her career, but even though she was attracted to spiritual things when she was a young girl, it wasn't until she was in graduate school that she came to understand what it meant to have a personal relationship with Jesus Christ.

She attended a Catholic school in Hong Kong because her mother thought faith-based schools provided a stronger education than the other available options. Her mother also thought religion was a crutch that a modern person did not need, but she gave Pin Pin permission to be baptized into the Catholic faith just before she graduated from high school. Shortly thereafter, Pin Pin left Hong Kong for the first time and embarked on a nineteen-day boat ride to San Francisco. From there, she road a bus to Coe College in Cedar Rapids, Iowa. Her goal: to see as much of the world as she could on her way to school in America.

"I took the boat because I could see Osaka, Tokyo, Hawaii, and San Francisco," she says. "And then I took the bus from San Francisco to Iowa because people said that buses stopped at, and railroads passed by, every city. I thought, *Okay, I want to stop at every city*, but I didn't realize that American cities are pretty much the same except for size."

Pin Pin quickly concluded that riding a bus was a horrible way to get across the country. Her misery mounted every time the bus stopped for a meal, usually at a Howard Johnson's restaurant. The first time she was confronted with an American menu, she was so confused she couldn't even order. The waitress, mistakenly judging by her youthful appearance that she was about twelve, suggested she have a hamburger, so that's what she ordered—at every stop. This only added to her discomfort; because Asian food is served fully flavored, she didn't even realize she needed to add salt or ketchup to her hamburgers. "I couldn't eat a single hamburger for three years after that," she says with a smile.

Finally, Pin Pin couldn't bear the thought of another tasteless hamburger, so she started waiting in the bus station during meal stops. "I'd sit in the depot worrying about whether I was missing my bus because I didn't know anything about these American cities or the American map," she says. "I didn't know which direction the buses were going, and I was trying to listen to make sure the one for Cedar Rapids did not leave without me. So I sat there and felt pretty confused, pretty much out of touch."

One day as she was waiting, she noticed a church across the street from the bus station. Lonely and desperately longing for a touch from God, Pin Pin walked over to the church and went into the sanctuary. The place was empty except for one lady cleaning the pews. Surprised to see an Asian visitor in her small town, the lady immediately asked Pin Pin where she was from. "That reminded me that I came from a very, very faraway place," she says. "I was already miserably tired, so I just started crying."

The lady kindly offered Pin Pin a shoulder to cry on, adding that she understood how her distraught young guest was feeling because she had seven children of her own. That struck a chord with Pin Pin, but it went deeper than the fact that she was one of seven children herself. "I thought, *Here is a place that is very different. I don't know a single soul, but God is here*," Pin Pin says. "I guess I saw that a mother's love was the same wherever I was and I thought, *I can survive in this country*. I decided then that if God was with me, then I could do it. That was probably the first time that God meant something to me personally—he was more than just the faith that was taught in my catechism training. He was no longer just the God that sits high up in heaven to judge all men."

Encouraged by the emotional understanding that God was with her, Pin Pin went through her first years of college as a devout Catholic. She attended mass at 6:30 every morning, and she faithfully adhered to her faith's dietary restriction of not eating meat—only fish—on Fridays. "I hated fish and sometimes I would even throw up after eating fried fish, but I would abide by it because I thought it would please God," she says.

But in her junior year, when the church abolished the "fish-on-Friday" rule, Pin Pin began to question her faith. She didn't understand how one man—the pope—could arbitrarily decide what she needed to do to have a right relationship with God. Her questions led her to take a course on comparative religion, and by the time she graduated from Coe College, she believed that there were many ways to heaven. *If God is love, and if God is fair*, she reasoned, *then if I live in an African jungle and never hear about him, will he condemn me to hell?* The obvious answer was no, Pin Pin concluded. And that was her spiritual state when she went to Yale.

There, she met a young woman from Indonesia named Helen. Helen, who was the happiest person Pin Pin had ever known, had a habit of punctuating everything she said with "Praise the Lord." This, plus her frequent references to Jesus Christ, really got on Pin Pin's nerves. So she took it upon herself to convince her fellow student how narrow-minded she was. "I had all these logical reasons why Jesus Christ couldn't be the only way," Pin Pin says. "He could be the best way, but he was not the only way."

Helen didn't change her mind, but neither could she think of how to refute Pin Pin's arguments. Instead, she recommended that when Pin Pin went home to New York (she commuted to school in New Haven, Connecticut), she look up a certain Bible study teacher, a friend of Helen's who might be able to tell her why Jesus Christ was the only way.

So the next time Pin Pin was in New York, she went to the home where the Bible study was held. "I have believed in God emotionally for many years," she told the teacher. "Now I need to know logically why Jesus Christ is the only way. Can you help me?"

The teacher tried his best, but although he explained the gospel to Pin Pin every time she came back to the Bible study, he could not persuade her to change her mind. Pin Pin also discussed her spiritual struggle with her husband, who was already a believer, but even he was unable to make her understand why the claims of Christianity were true.

Finally, the Bible study teacher asked his wife, who was not part of the group, to pray for Pin Pin. "The more she prayed, the more I got depressed," Pin Pin remembers. "I could not understand why at this stage of my life I felt that way. I was going to one of the best schools in the country; I was doing well at school; I was married to the man I loved; I had no financial problems, no health problems, no family problems, no academic problems. Then why was I so unhappy?"

After analyzing the situation, Pin Pin realized that her relationship with God was the only area of her life that was not settled. "I said, 'Okay, Jesus Christ, I don't understand why you are the only one, but I am too tired to fight. I am going to put down my weapon and you will have to show me afterward why you are the only way.'"

As Pin Pin and her husband prayed together, she felt as if a ton of weight had just lifted from her shoulders. "I went back to the Bible study on Friday and told this man to tell his wife that she didn't need to pray for me anymore," Pin Pin says. "I told him that I took it by faith that Christ is the only way."

Following God's Lead

By the time Pin Pin began her banking career several years later, she was firmly grounded in her faith and cognizant of the need to incorporate her relationship with Christ into her work. As she progressed through the ranks in the banking world, she grew increasingly aware that God would lead her where he wanted her to go, and that when he opened a door, she needed to go through it.

After seventeen years with her first employer, Pin Pin was offered a job as chief lending officer at a community bank in Manhattan. Six months later, she became the chief operating officer, and then six months after that, she was named CEO. The bank had a troubled history, but Pin Pin was able to get it on the right track. "I turned it around so well that the owner who had been stuck with it for some years thought that this was a good time to sell," she says.

He sold it to a person who, when the bank was struggling, had tried to buy it several times for next to nothing. This particular buyer had gone to great lengths to get the bank that way, but as CEO, Pin Pin thwarted his efforts every time. He had finally agreed to pay what Pin Pin knew to be a fair price. Although the purchase agreement stipulated that there would be no change in management, Pin Pin's previous struggles with the buyer made her question whether she wanted to work for him. "At that point, my feeling was that if God wanted me to stay, then I had the faith to stay," she says. "But if God wanted me to go, I would go wherever he sent me."

A week before the owner of the bank called Pin Pin to tell her he was selling the bank, she had noticed a large classified advertisement in the *American Banker* newspaper. A bank—it didn't say which one—was seeking a president and CEO. "I thought, *That's curious; most banks don't look for a CEO by putting an advertisement in a newspaper,*" Pin Pin says. "The ad said, 'Only someone with a successful track record and experience in commercial lending, international trade finance, and working with Asian customers would be desirable.' That sounded like my résumé. That's the reason the ad made an impression on me, even though I was sitting pretty in my job, I was making a very nice profit, and the world was beautiful."

When the owner of her bank called Pin Pin to tell her about his plans to sell, she remembered the ad she had seen. When she hung up, she asked her secretary to gather the previous week's newspapers. "Usually those newspapers got circulated and they were gone," Pin Pin says. "But she found the paper that had the advertisement in it, so I sent my résumé for the fun of it."

Pin Pin was not at home when a representative from the search firm that had placed the ad called looking for "Mr. Chau." Her husband, who is a scientist, not a banker, quickly pointed out that it was his wife who had sent in the résumé. "There was silence on the other end because they were expecting a man," Pin Pin says. "That's the convenience of having a name that is not gender-specific in English—people assume that it is a man's name!"

The search firm representative said he would call back, but Pin Pin assumed she'd never hear from him again. A few days later, however, he called her at her office and began to tell her about the job at Summit National Bank. "That is when I found out it was in Atlanta," she says. "I had never thought about going to Atlanta. I got out a map and found that Georgia is only one state north of Florida. We're talking about the *Deep* South!"

Although Pin Pin had never dreamed of moving so far away, she had told God that she would go through any door that he opened. The opportunity in Atlanta looked like a wide-open door, so she decided to go down for an interview.

Pin Pin and her husband liked Atlanta, but they knew that moving there would be a radical step for them. They didn't know anything about the city, and they didn't have any friends there. There also was Raymond's job to think about, and the needs of their only child, a daughter who was in college at the time. "We thought we had better be sure that this was where God wanted us to be," Pin Pin says. "So we set out for ourselves three criteria, and if all three of them were met, then we would know the move was God's will. Some were common sense—the job had to offer compensation that would make it worthwhile to me. But we did set one criteria that, unless God intervened, wouldn't happen, and we had to negotiate for three months before it was finally delivered. That's when I realized that this was where God wanted me to be."

When Pin Pin went to work for Summit in 1993, the bank was five years old. It had total assets of $80 million, and it had just finished its first profitable year. Although the bank was trending upward financially, it was in desperate need of some stable leadership as it had gone through three chief executives in its short history. "This was a bank with a lot of talent and energy but the staff was not focused," Pin Pin says. "In fact, as in many banks in that particular stage of development, the people did not always see eye to eye as to how things needed to be run." Pin Pin was about to change that.

Challenges of Leadership

In the years since, the bank's total assets have increased by $240 million. With growth come greater responsibility and visibility—and greater pressure to meet other people's expectations. Pin Pin's faith has helped her deal with these added burdens. She says that the fact that she is a follower of Christ gives her confidence that she would not have otherwise: "My security does not come from what the board thinks about me, or what my employees think about me. As a CEO you cannot please everybody. You have to make decisions that some people may not be happy about."

It's easy for people to become more insecure as they rise through the ranks in an organization, Pin Pin believes. They are bound to have subordinates who would love to be in their position, and those colleagues might be willing to do anything to get there. But because Pin Pin is secure in her position—both at the bank and in her relationship with Christ—she doesn't hesitate to give her employees the latitude they need to do their best. "I don't have to worry about what their motive is or wonder if they are going to shoot me in the back. I feel that if God wants me to be where I am, then he has a reason for it, and until he wants me elsewhere, no one can get me out of here," she says.

It can be lonely at the top. Senior executives like Pin Pin can't readily share their struggles and fears about running a company because whatever they say might end up on the corporate grapevine. As she makes difficult decisions and deals with sensitive issues, Pin Pin draws great strength from the words of God she finds in the Book of Isaiah. When she finds herself needing to make a tough personnel decision, for example, she takes comfort in Isaiah 49:16, where God says, "See, I have engraved you on the palms of my hands."

"Sometimes you make decisions that affect other people's lives," Pin Pin says. "You may need to tell an employee, 'I'm sorry, but it didn't work out. You need to find a different place to work.' There is a side of you that is the responsible side: you are hired to do a job, you answer to a group of shareholders and other employees, so you must do the thing that is fair. Yet there is a part of you that is soft and compassionate, and when you lay someone off, it's difficult. So sometimes you need that embrace from God that says, 'You're okay.'"

It can be tempting for a leader to put too much stock into what other people think, particularly at critical decision points. "There have been so many times that I was afraid about the decisions that I alone needed to make," Pin Pin admits. "A CEO's job comes with a lot of risk premium. I face situations that have consequences that are more drastic than, say, when I was in a less responsible position. When you are in a lower echelon within the company and you make a mistake, it's not as visible as when a CEO makes the mistake."

At times like this, Pin Pin is reminded of Isaiah 51:12–13, which says:

> I, even I, am he who comforts you.
>> Who are you that you fear mortal men,
>> the sons of men, who are but grass,
> that you forget the LORD your Maker,
>> who stretched out the heavens
>> and laid the foundations of the earth,
> that you live in constant terror every day
>> because of the wrath of the oppressor,
>> who is bent on destruction?
> For where is the wrath of the oppressor?

This passage was especially meaningful to Pin Pin at a point in her career when she stood up for a colleague who wasn't being treated fairly by a new division manager. Pin Pin was getting ready to accompany the CEO of the bank to Asia, and when her colleague heard about her upcoming trip, he begged her to talk to the executive about his problem. "I did the politically stupid thing," she says. "When I traveled with the CEO and he made a comment about how bright and kind this new division manager was, I said, 'He could be very bright, but I don't know if he's kind.' I began to tell how unprofessionally this colleague of mine was being treated."

Wanting to improve the situation, the CEO spoke to the division manager about the problem. The manager was able to trace the comments back to Pin Pin. "From that time on, I became a target," she says. "He made sure that life was miserable for me because I spoke 'evil' about him."

Years later, after Pin Pin went to work for the community bank and began dealing with the prospective buyer who wanted to get the bank for much less than its value, she began to understand why God had allowed her to go through the ringer with that division manager. "It taught me not to fear men," she says. "In the twelve years I've been CEO, I have found that if I act out of conviction, after prayerful consideration, then I can sit and wait for God to vindicate me. And God has been very gracious. I get my strength through knowing his Word and knowing that his unfailing love will always be there for me. It will not be shaken."

A Responsible Witness

Although many of the people with whom Pin Pin works know she is a woman of faith, she is careful not to use her position to force her beliefs on anyone in the company. "I understand that there is a different weight to what a CEO says and what a rank-and-file person says," she explains. "When I was a rank-and-filer, I could be more vocal and people would not take offense. But as a CEO, what I say would be interpreted differently."

For example, she has prayer groups at some of Summit's branches, including one that meets on Thursday mornings in her own office. But when one branch wanted to hold the meeting over the lunch break, she insisted that the prayer sessions occur only before work-hours. "I don't want nonbelievers to think that because the president is a Christian, Christians have special rights," she says. "For example, if they should linger longer on their lunch hour, it would look as if I were giving them preferential treatment. I think that this is also part of the Christian testimony, that Christians need to be on time for work."

As Pin Pin has matured and assumed positions of greater responsibility, she has come to believe that sharing her faith has less to do with what she says with her mouth and more to do with what she does with her life. "I try to be faithful to what I perceive is the Christian principle and live it on a day-to-day basis," she says. "When I was younger and in a lesser position, I probably used my lips more than I used my life."

Pin Pin doesn't hesitate to pray with employees who are going through difficult times. But she has learned the importance of not being flippant about discussing her faith at work. One December, it became obvious that Summit National Bank was not going to meet its budget for that year. Hoping that God would somehow intervene, Pin Pin told another bank executive that she was praying that they would be able to reach their financial target. His response? "No amount of prayer will help!"

Pin Pin insisted that it would, and the two decided to bet on it. The loser of the bet had to wear shorts and stand in the bank parking lot for an hour—in January! Convinced that Pin Pin was going to lose, her colleague even went so far as to give her a gift in the middle of an officers' meeting: a pair of men's black boxer shorts covered with big yellow "yucky" faces. Looking back, Pin Pin readily admits that making such a bet was a silly thing to do: "God did not want me to be backing him into such a corner. It wasn't a wise thing to do. No amount of prayer would change the shortage in the budget."

Pin Pin lost the bet. She kept her end of the bargain, though. She put on those ugly boxers, stood in the parking lot for an hour beginning at 6 A.M., and then went to her officers' meeting at 8 A.M.—still wearing the boxers. "I think most people didn't think I would do that," she says, smiling. "But I said, 'Hey, look, I need to be in good spirits.' I didn't want the whole world to see me in men's boxer shorts in the parking lot because we didn't meet the budget. But I did it. If I lose the bet, I lose. I did a stupid thing, and I had to suffer the stupid consequences!"

Speaking Out

While Pin Pin usually lives her faith quietly at work, she is quite vocal about it in her frequent presentations to professional organizations and other groups in the Atlanta area. She realizes that although some people would never darken the door of a church, they might be inclined to listen to her because of her position in the business world. So when invited to speak, Pin Pin nearly always accepts. "I think it is my responsibility," she explains. "I think that God wants me to be, in whatever small part, his mouthpiece to a group of people who may not want to go to a church and listen to a sermon. So even if I am very busy, I say yes to invitations to speak unless I know for sure I would not have an opportunity to talk about my personal faith."

Pin Pin is careful to note for the audience that her speech has not been sanctioned by her company or by the person who invited her to speak. She doesn't tell people that they have to become followers of Christ, but she does address issues such as balance from a Christ-centered perspective. Pin Pin talks about the fact that God made people with a body, a soul, and a spirit, and that to have proper balance, all three must be in order. (The soul, as she defines it, is a person's emotional and mental side, while the spirit has to do with the spiritual side.) She points out that people often don't have to be told to care for their bodies and their souls, but they often fail to tend to their spirits. "The spirit is your connection to eternity," she tells them, "and as a Christian, I believe that Christ is the bridge to eternity. After you have your structure right, you can relax. If you take care of those basic structures, you can open yourself to all opportunities in life, and then you'll find a very pleasing result at the end."

While Pin Pin knows that the people who invite her to speak might not expect her to talk about her faith, she doesn't hesitate to share how she came to know Christ or the difference that he has made in her life. "If I tell them the story about my coming to America, most people do not consider it offensive, and yet God is in it," she says. "It's genuine. I'm not telling people a lie or making up a story—it actually happened, and it has had long-term influence in my life."

Pin Pin finds that her speeches are generally well received: "Usually after I speak I get letters from people that tell me it ministered to them, they needed that particular message at that time, or they think it is refreshing that a person in the business community will come out and speak about her faith."

No "Clumps"

Back at the office, Pin Pin strives to carry out her daily responsibilities in a way that fulfills the biblical mandate to be salt and light. And she has a definite opinion on how this should be done: "To me, to be salt is to be mixed with the ordinary—people will know that there is something different. But the Bible doesn't tell us to be a clump of salt. In-your-face Christian witnessing is a clump of salt that doesn't do anything but put a bad taste in people's mouths. I definitely believe in a brand of Christian witness that is more low profile, more minding my own business, living my own Christian life so that others will see the light that I reflect. We can be only reflectors of light, not the source of light."

Being a good worker is one way to be effective for Christ while avoiding the tendency to be an offensive witness, Pin Pin says. "People think that they have to be good Christians first, then good workers, but I think it's the other way around. If you're not a good worker, you cannot have the respect of your colleagues, and then how could they respect your faith? If your faith is not making you live a model life, then why would they need it?

"I think the most effective Christian witness is when people have to ask, 'Why is this person different? Why is this person more peaceful? Why is this person more secure? Why is this person so responsive? It's because of this person's faith. This is what makes her tick.' If it's something attractive, other people might want it too."

If followers of Christ in the marketplace aren't comfortable expressing their faith vocally, they should at least be aware of their actions so that they don't become a stumbling block to anyone else, Pin Pin believes. She became very aware of this danger at a particularly trying time in her career. During her tenure with her first employer, she was the manager of commercial lending at one of the bank's branches. When her boss, the branch manager, left, she and the operations manager began sharing the leadership duties. This didn't go over well with the operations manager, who wanted to be the only top person at the branch.

But his results didn't match his desire. After the branch manager left, the operations side of the bank went downhill, while the commercial lending side—which Pin Pin oversaw—flourished. So naturally, she thought she should be in charge of the office. As Pin Pin and the operations manager battled for control, their obvious lack of harmony had a negative impact on the environment at the office. "It was difficult for people to work under us, especially when the assistant manager was fanning the fire," she says.

Pin Pin's irritation at her colleague continued until one day, she realized that her actions could keep him from responding if one day he heard the gospel. "So I decided to take the initiative and offer peace," she says. "I have to tell you that at this point, his being a Christian was the remotest thing on earth. There wasn't anything that would point him in that direction, and I certainly hadn't been an instrument of grace. But at some point the Holy Spirit spoke to me and said, 'Pin Pin, do you want to be the stumbling block for this person when one day he should be presented with the opportunity to know Christ?' I said, 'Lord, I don't want to be the stumbling block.' So I went to him with peace, and from that time on we stopped the fighting."

The operations manager eventually resigned, and Pin Pin was put in charge of the entire branch. But the story doesn't end there. About fifteen years later, after Pin Pin had moved to Atlanta and the operations manager had moved to California, the two happened to bump into each other while they were both visiting Chinatown in New York. "He was very happy," she says. "He knew I was Christian, and the first thing he told me was, 'Pin Pin, I have become a Christian.'"

As Pin Pin listened to her old nemesis tell about how Christ had changed his life, she was overwhelmed with gratefulness that she had obeyed God so many years earlier. "I'm not saying that my heeding the Holy Spirit made him a Christian," she says. "But when I saw that I had not been an impediment to his believing, I was happy that God let me hear the entire story."

When Pin Pin was navigating rough terrain early on in her career, she only wanted God to remove her from the problems. She didn't consider that she would one day look back and realize that she had grown from them and that good had actually come from them. But now, after more than three decades in the banking business, she can be a bit more circumspect about the tough times. "When I look back, I understand why all these things happened," she says. "I see that God has pulled all these pieces together to accomplish something. Now that's always my perspective: that I'm always a work in progress. I don't know what the Maker is going to make out of me. But to the extent that I can, I will try not to fight it and allow him to mold me, and guide me, and make me whatever he wants to make me."

Afterword

WHILE READING ABOUT THE WOMEN IN THIS BOOK, you may have thought, *I wish I could ask Carmen about* . . . or *I wonder what Bonnie thinks about* . . . Well, here's your chance. They've all graciously given us permission to share their e-mail addresses precisely so you can contact them if you'd like to engage in dialogue.

Here they are:

Susie Case: spcase@yahoo.com
Pin Pin Chau: PinPinChau@aol.com
Karen Covell: jkcmusic@earthlink.net
Joyce Godwin: JoyceGodwin@compuserve.com
Allyson Hodgins: caird@connect.ab.ca
Carmen Jones: cjones@disability-marketing.com
Dr. Sally Knox: officesknox@aol.com
Goldie Rotenberg: lox2@earthlink.net
Jeanette Towne: jtowne@townetalk.com
Bonnie Wurzbacher: Bwurzbacher@aol.com

Furthermore, if you have feedback on the overall content of the book, please e-mail me at lflowers@lifeatwork.com, or write to me at The Life@Work Co., P.O. Box 1928, Fayetteville, AR 72702. Let the conversation begin!

Appendix A
KEY LEARNINGS

TEN INTENSE INTERVIEWS, EACH CONDUCTED in person, each lasting several hours. Pages and pages of single-spaced, typed notes, all brimming with enough insights and anecdotes to fill several books. There were times during this project when I suffered more from information overload than I did from writer's block.

Writing this book was an educational experience unlike any I've had in my life. Not only did I learn about the personal histories of ten women (an amazing process by itself), but I also had the opportunity to soak up the wisdom they have garnered during their many collective years in the marketplace.

The beauty of a book like this is that each person who reads it will be touched by it in different ways, and each will come away with her own set of learnings. There isn't enough space left in this book to record every lesson I learned, but in these last few pages, I've captured a few highlights.

First Things First

- A growing, thriving personal relationship with Jesus Christ—nurtured through daily Bible reading, prayer, and meditation—is vitally important for a person who wants to integrate faith and work successfully.

- No matter, work related or otherwise, is too small to present to God in prayer.

- It's helpful to have a "spiritual board of directors"—a group of friends who can offer professional advice as well as prayer support.

- These few close friends should be free to speak into every area of my life—from my relationship with Christ to my work schedule—and to let me know when I'm getting off track.

Women and Work

- Not all women fit the same mold; God calls each woman to do and be something different.

- There's no direct command or one-size-fits-all answer in the Bible about whether married women with children should work outside the home. The question often comes down to motive: would I be *willing* to give up my career if God were to call me to stay at home?

- People often assume that successful women in business who don't have children have *chosen* not to have children, but often that is not the case at all.

Competence

- As a follower of Christ, I can combat my professional insecurities with the knowledge that my confidence comes from God, not from my own strength or abilities. I should strive to do my best, but ultimately, God's opinion of me is the only one that matters.

- Work is a powerful witness, and by establishing myself as extremely competent in my profession, I make it difficult for the people with whom I interact to doubt my credibility when they learn that I'm a follower of Christ.

Calling

- The place where I am the most effective for God is where my gifts, my passions, and my success overlap.

- I can't allow myself to fall into the trap of believing that I have to do everything well or that I have to be all things to all people. Instead, I need to figure out what my gifts are and develop them.

- God won't call me to a particular job or field without equipping me with the tools I need to do it.

Trusting God

- If I firmly believe that God has put me in a particular job or position, I must have faith that when things don't go the way I want them to, he has me there for a reason.

- When God shows up unexpectedly, that experience becomes the thing that I fall back on when my faith begins to sag again.

- When God closes a door, it's because he knows what's best and he has something else for me to do. Instead of trying to break down the door or becoming angry and resentful, I need to find other ways to serve him.

- God is gracious, and he doesn't put challenges in front of me before I'm ready to handle them. The key is to trust in him and not in myself.

- It's easy to play with "what-ifs"—to wonder what might have happened if I had grown up in a different city or gone to a different college or studied another major. Such mental gymnastics are interesting, but as a believer, all I can do is make decisions based on prayer, godly counsel, and Scripture, and then trust that God will direct my path.

Salt and Light

- The Bible calls believers to be salt and light, but it doesn't call me to be a clump of salt. Too much salt only puts a bad taste in people's mouths; it does nothing to draw others closer to Jesus.

- I don't have to hand out tracts or hold Bible studies in the corporate cafeteria to share my faith with people at work. Living in such a way that allows people to see Jesus in me can be a powerful witness.

- Those people who have an authentic relationship with Christ—and who live it out in a gentle, nonabrasive manner on a daily basis—often are the ones to whom coworkers turn when they have problems.

- A willingness to talk about tragic or painful things in my own life can open doors to conversations that might never happen if I keep talk on a strictly business level.

Integrity

- One of the most effective ways to be a light for Christ at work is to approach all aspects of my job with integrity. But I must be very careful not to make moral issues out of things that are really simply preferences, business risk issues, or philosophical differences.

- Coworkers who are not believers don't always have the same moral and ethical standards as I do, nor should I expect them to. I may believe very strongly in the biblical concept of avoiding the appearance of evil, but that doesn't mean that I should force everyone else to adhere to my way of doing things.

- The misery of compromise is a lot worse than the misery that can accompany standing up for what I believe.

- If I ever get to the point where I feel I cannot leave a job or a certain position, especially if I'm in a job that pays a lot or has really good benefits, then I'm setting myself up for compromise. And small compromises generally lead to bigger ones.

• Making right ethical choices becomes easier over time as I gain experience and confidence in both my abilities and my faith.

Relationships with Coworkers

• Everyone has a story. My coworker might be the most bitter, angry, or unpleasant person I've ever known, but there's a reason for it. I may never know what that reason is, but just realizing there's probably more to it than meets the eye often makes dealing with that person easier.

• A sense of humor is a key survival tool for a follower of Christ in today's marketplace. It comes in handy when dealing with difficult people and when taking an ethical stand, as well as during the day-to-day struggles of work.

Balancing Life's Demands

• When I'm up to my eyeballs in work, it's very easy to say, "Once I meet this deadline, I'll slow down." Unfortunately, once that deadline passes, another one usually is looming on the horizon. It becomes a never-ending process unless I'm intentional about getting some balance in my life.

• One of the best ways to keep work from taking over my whole life is to get organized. This adds structure to my life (which in turn brings freedom) and forces other people to plan ahead, thus avoiding the kind of last-minute crises that cause stress and anxiety for everyone involved.

• Many women who are not employed outside the home deal with the "guilt" of not earning an income by saying yes to anyone who needs help. As a result, many such women are busier and more stressed out than they would be if they had full-time jobs.

- Learning to say no is a key element of a balanced life, with or without a paycheck.

- Single women without children may be more vulnerable to overload than working mothers because of other people's perception that because they don't have family obligations, they have plenty of time for extracurricular activities.

- To avoid burnout, all women need to be honest about how much downtime they need. If I don't take care of my needs first, I will be less effective at helping others.

- God is a God of order, calm, and peace. If I am leading a frenetic life, I'm likely not going to make anybody want what I have in terms of a relationship with Christ.

Appendix B
MEANINGFUL PASSAGES

EACH WOMAN INTERVIEWED FOR THIS BOOK was asked to share Scripture passages that have helped her meld her faith into her work life. The following is a compilation of many of these verses, grouped by topics that are relevant to the integration process. This is not intended to be a comprehensive list; it is merely a starting point for people who wish to incorporate biblical wisdom into their work life.

Ambition
Seek first his kingdom and his righteousness, and all these things will be given to you as well. (Matt. 6:33)

Avoiding negativity
Glorify the LORD with me;
   let us exalt his name together. (Ps. 34:3)

Battling stress and anxiety
Do not be anxious about anything, but in everything, by prayer and petition, with thanksgiving, present your requests to God. And the peace of God, which transcends all understanding, will guard your hearts and your minds in Christ Jesus. (Phil. 4:6–7)

Comfort in tough times
See, I have engraved you on the palms of my hands. (Isa. 49:16)

"Though the mountains be shaken
  and the hills be removed,
yet my unfailing love for you will not be shaken
  nor my covenant of peace be removed,"
  says the LORD, who has compassion on you. (Isa. 54:10)

Courage

I, even I, am he who comforts you.
  Who are you that you fear mortal men,
  the sons of men, who are but grass,
that you forget the LORD your Maker,
  who stretched out the heavens
  and laid the foundations of the earth,
that you live in constant terror every day
  because of the wrath of the oppressor,
  who is bent on destruction?
For where is the wrath of the oppressor?
  The cowering prisoners will soon be set free;
they will not die in their dungeon,
  nor will they lack bread.
For I am the LORD your God,
  who churns up the sea so that its waves roar—
  the LORD Almighty is his name. (Isa. 51:12–15)

Developing and using gifts

We have different gifts, according to the grace given us. If a man's gift is prophesying, let him use it in proportion to his faith. If it is serving, let him serve; if it is teaching, let him teach; if it is encouraging, let him encourage; if it is contributing to the needs of others, let him give generously; if it is leadership, let him govern diligently; if it is showing mercy, let him do it cheerfully. (Rom. 12:6–8)

Excellence

Whatever you do, whether in word or deed, do it all in the name of the Lord Jesus, giving thanks to God the Father through him. (Col. 3:17)

Whatever you do, work at it with all your heart, as working for the Lord, not for men, since you know that you will receive an inheritance from the Lord as a reward. It is the Lord Christ you are serving. (Col. 3:23–24)

Fellowship

Let us not give up meeting together, as some are in the habit of doing, but let us encourage one another—and all the more as you see the Day approaching. (Heb. 10:25)

Financial stewardship

The rich rule over the poor,
and the borrower is a servant to the lender. (Prov. 22:7)

"Bring the whole tithe into the storehouse, that there may be food in my house. Test me in this," says the LORD Almighty, "and see if I will not throw open the floodgates of heaven and pour out so much blessing that you will not have room enough for it." (Mal. 3:10)

Flexibility

O LORD, you are our Father.
We are the clay, you are the potter;
we are all the work of your hand. (Isa. 64:8)

God orchestrates our careers

Who knows but that you have come to royal position for such a time as this? (Esther 4:14)

"For I know the plans I have for you," declares the LORD, "plans to prosper you and not to harm you, plans to give you hope and a future." (Jer. 29:11)

Integrity

Above all else, guard your heart,
for it is the wellspring of life. (Prov. 4:23)

A good name is more desirable than great riches;
to be esteemed is better than silver or gold. (Prov. 22:1)

Whatever is true, whatever is noble, whatever is right, whatever is pure, whatever is lovely, whatever is admirable—if anything is excellent or praiseworthy—think about such things. Whatever you have learned or received or heard from me, or seen in me—put it into practice. And the God of peace will be with you. (Phil. 4:8–9)

Partnerships

Do not be yoked together with unbelievers. For what do righteousness and wickedness have in common? Or what fellowship can light have with darkness? (2 Cor. 6:14)

Relationships with coworkers

A heart at peace gives life to the body,
   but envy rots the bones. (Prov. 14:30)

The fruit of the Spirit is love, joy, peace, patience, kindness, goodness, faithfulness, gentleness and self-control. Against such things there is no law. (Gal. 5:22–23)

Sharing faith

If you confess with your mouth, "Jesus is Lord," and believe in your heart that God raised him from the dead, you will be saved. (Rom. 10:9)

I pray that you may be active in sharing your faith, so that you will have a full understanding of every good thing we have in Christ. (Philem. 6)

Time

Show me, O LORD, my life's end
   and the number of my days;
   let me know how fleeting is my life. (Ps. 39:4)

Trusting God

Trust in the LORD with all your heart
   and lean not on your own understanding;
   in all your ways acknowledge him,
   and he will make your paths straight. (Prov. 3:5–6)

Jesus said, "Did I not tell you that if you believed, you would see the glory of God?" (John 11:40)

We know that in all things God works for the good of those who love him, who have been called according to his purpose. (Rom. 8:28)

Wisdom

She is a tree of life to those who embrace her;
those who lay hold of her will be blessed. (Prov. 3:18)

Notes

Chapter 8

1. Goldie Rotenberg, "Goldie: Could God Reach a Girl on the Top of the World?" *The Chosen People*, February 1986, 6.
2. Stephen J. Dubner, *Turbulent Souls* (New York: Avon Books, Inc., 1998), 300.

About the Author

WITH A DEGREE IN JOURNALISM FROM John Brown University, Lois Flowers has spent much of her professional life covering business news for print media. Prior to joining the Life@Work Company in 1998 as assistant editor of *The Life@Work Journal*, she was a business writer with the Arkansas Democrat-Gazette. Now senior writer for Life@Work, Lois lives near Fayetteville, Arkansas, with her husband, Randy.

BLENDING BIBLICAL WISDO

A Life@Work Book

THE LIFE@WORK BOOK

SIXTEEN RESPECTED LEADERS TALK ABOUT
BLENDING BIBLICAL WISDOM AND BUSINESS EXCELLENCE

The award-winning *Life@Work* magazine is dedicated to blending biblical wisdom and marketplace excellence. Now, for the first time, *Life@Work* brings together the most intriguing and insightful writings of their contributors in one incredible volume: *The Life@Work Book*. Join Larry Burkett, Laurie Beth Jones, Os Guiness, Charles Swindoll, and other leading Christian writers in the further integration of spiritual life at work.

A Life@Work Book

THE FOURTH FRONTIER

EXPLORING THE NEW WORLD OF WORK

STEPHEN GRAVES AND
THOMAS ADDINGTON

Unlike other God-ordained institutions—church, family, and government—followers of Christ routinely treat work as a necessity; something
we must do to make a living, a separate and disconnected entity of
existence. Addington and Graves show that work, in fact, is ordained by
God. By exploring such landscapes as calling, devotion, stewardship,
influence, integrity, and rest, readers can discover how to have a Kingdom
influence in the marketplace while living an integrated life in the
Fourth Frontier.

WORD PUBLISHING